Aug 2011

Jake

enjoy!

Ry—

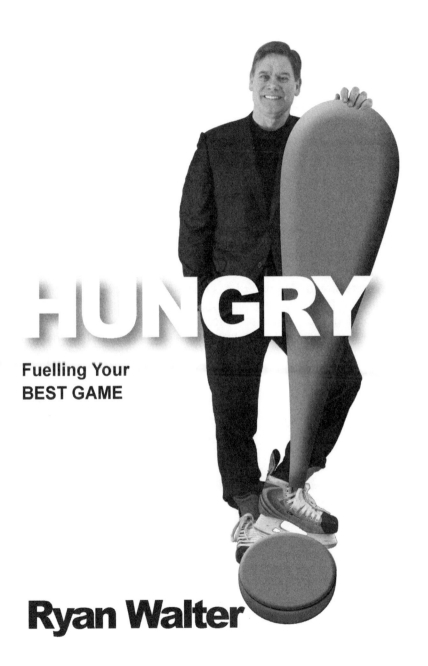

HUNGRY

**Fuelling Your
BEST GAME**

Ryan Walter

HUNGRY

Fuelling your BEST GAME

By: Ryan Walter

Published by: Heads-Up Communications Corp.

www.ryanwalter.com
www.hungryfuellingyourbestgame.com

Softcover ISBN: 978-0-9869281-0-9
Hardcover ISBN: 978-0-9869281-1-6

Printed in the U.S.

First Edition, May 2011

Edited by: Jennifer Walter
Interior layout by: Rod Schulhauser
Graphics by: Ryan Michael Harrison Walter
Cover Photo by: Jorge Parra
Cover design by: Rod Schulhauser
Project Management by: Rod Schulhauser

Dedication

I dedicate this book to my loved ones who help to keep me *hungry*.

My mother and father, Bill and Viona live life with such priority around family, giving to others, and integrity. They have inspired my *hungry spirit* throughout my life. And I cherish the friendship of Jenn's folks, George and Florence.

My brothers, George and Brent, and my sister Donna, remain close to me. Thanks for the times together around the pool with all the kids! Jenn's sisters, Wendy and Shelley and their families, though far away, are amazingly close in spirit.

Every one of our children ignites my *hungry spirit*, through who they are and how they live out their lives. Emma is my little jewel. She brightens my life with her smile, smarts and warmth. The way our Joe respects and connects with people teaches me to have a soft, kind heart, even when wronged. Ryan's passion for life encourages me to risk more and be all that I can be. Christi's giving presence and conversation reminds me to live with enthusiasm. Ben's integrity, focus, and resilience inspire my own.

Finally, to my wife Jenni Jingles:

Jenni, you are my best friend, my love, and my life partner. I can't wait to have coffee with you early every morning. Not only do you inspire my *hungry spirit*, but you write it into my life, daily. Jenn, you are my trusted editor, and I could not have written this book or lived this *hungry* life without you!

Contents

Acknowledgements

There are so many to thank. So many friends, colleagues, mentors, and teammates have invested in my life. I would like to publicly acknowledge my gratitude to those I have listed below and beg the forgiveness of those whom my 5 concussions have caused me to momentarily forget.

A big thanks to Brian Tracy for his endorsement of *Hungry* and for the content he has generated. I have been a big fan for over 20 years!

I want to thank Jamie MacDonald and his company Maximum Impact for our brainstorming times about Leadership.

Thank-you Ray Tudino, for being such a valuable participant in the first Ryan Walter Leadership Cruise, and thank you so very much for your support for *Hungry!* in the foreword to this book.

I would like to thank my friend and mentor Rick Matishak for our performance/leadership brainstorms and for the hands-on opportunity he gave me to learn alongside him.

My prof and friend, Matt Logan has moved me further down the road toward completion with every conversation we have had.

My good friend, Garth Froese sharpens my *hungry spirit* and has provided countless innovative suggestions and ideas and prompted many more.

Mike Gartner, far away in miles, is always close in heart issues.

My friend, Dan Loney and I have discussed *Hungry* for years, challenging one another all the while.

Rod Schulhauser brought this book together.

Our gifted son, Ryan Michael Harrison Walter created the graphics.

A big thanks to Mike McEwan at Grump Media for all his energy towards making our online connection work so well.

Sean Richardson provided wonderful feedback around my *Hungry* Model™.

Mike Johnston, my friend and co-author on the *Simply Series*, and *Hockey Plays and Strategies*, has kept my writing well-practiced.

Bill Stanley's faith in God during his fight with cancer is a dazzling demonstration of *Rebounding*.

To each of my many teammates: you taught me about playing *hungry*.

To all the Vancouver Canucks players I coached: together we learned how to be a *hungry* team.

To every member of the Canadian National Women's Hockey Team: you are among the best in the world and *hungry* to be even better.

Foreword

I am a First Sergeant.
My job is people-Every One is my Business.
I dedicate my time and energy to their needs,
Their health, morale, discipline and welfare.
I grow in strength
by strengthening my people.
My job is done in faith;
my people build my faith.
The Air Force is my life;
I share it with my people.
I believe in the Air Force goal-
"We take care of our own."
My job is people-
EVERY ONE IS MY BUSINESS

Definition of leadership from a military perspective: "Leadership is the art of influencing and directing people to accomplish the mission."

Ryan, based on the above creed which I, as a First Sergeant, live by and use to conduct my daily interactions with people, and referencing the military's definition of leadership, you can see how the content of your latest book directly applies to what I try to do with everyone I come into contact with.

As I read *Hungry* and worked through the exercises, it was evidently clear to me that the material you deliver matches something we work to develop in what we call *first line supervisors* – they are not upper management, owner's groups, or the board of directors, but they supervise our youngest Airmen every day and develop them into the next generation of leaders that will carry our Air Force to even greater achievements. If we were to reserve this development of the "Hungry Spirit" only for the highest levels, we would not be the greatest Air Force in the world.

The thought that resounded through my head as I considered what to provide as a short comment for your book is this – as a military leader my role is to develop, strengthen, and promote the "Hungry Spirit" within my organization and people for complete mission accomplishment.

The techniques provided in *Hungry! –Fuelling Your Best Game* provide me with additional tools to develop the Airmen –sons and daughters, husbands and wives, brothers and sisters – under my charge to their fullest potential.

Because, in the Military, there is no other alternative but to Win – this is my passion and purpose.

Ray Tudino
First Sergeant, US Air force

Warm-Up

What Does it Mean to be *Hungry*?

I spent 17 seasons of my life in the world of professional sport. It was an intense and competitive sandbox. Lessons there are learned and applied quickly, or management brings in someone else to learn them. The road I took to develop into one of the top 700 players in the world inclined up a steep learning curve, along which the pressure to "make it" had the potential to shape my character or crush my spirit.

What does it take to perform at the highest level? All recent research suggests that 10,000 hours of focused practice is a given, but there is a need to go much deeper. There are inner fuels that drive the best in the world to not only survive, but eventually fall in love with this arduous process.

President Ronald Reagan said, in his Inaugural Speech of Jan 20th 1981, "No arsenal is so formidable as the will and moral courage of free men and women." Over a century before Abraham Lincoln had advised: "Always bear in mind that your own resolution to succeed is more important than any one thing." And cosmetic giant Mary Kay Ash has since added: "The only difference between successful people and unsuccessful people is extraordinary determination."

While many books talk about performance, few focus specifically on what these three leaders were trying to tell us. There is a mysterious, universally-available inner energy that feeds all high performance. This is what HUNGRY is all about!

What Does it Mean to be un-Hungry (and is it even a word)?

My family and I recently visited the Rock and Roll Hall of Fame in Cleveland Ohio. While taking time out to purchase a coffee on the 3rd floor of the 6-storey building, I asked the young cashier serving me, "What is your favourite part of this amazing exhibit?"

Without pausing, this thirty-something man flatly answered, "The EXIT sign."

> "Your ability to keep your fire burning in the midst of a storm is paramount to becoming a champion."
>
> **Dan Green**

How sad... this employee was surrounded by the stories and music of inspiring artists, the best of the best, and all he wanted to do was leave. Meanwhile, up on the 5th floor I listened to the amazing Bruce Springsteen, whose recorded voice spoke about "not wanting to do anything casual in life," but instead "desiring deeply to do something great."

Many people get rocked by the circumstances of life and then wallow in mediocrity. Do you and I want to just exist to exit... or do we deeply desire to find ways to be our very best? The difference between these two extremes is the personal tension I call the *hungry spirit*.

You're FIRED!

Let me ask you a personal question... have you ever been fired? Or, have you ever experienced:
- Job loss?
- Difficult times?
- Health problems?

- Broken relationships?
- Playing on an under-performing team?
- Trying to lead disengaged workers?
- Extreme disappointment caused by people close to you?

If you have a heartbeat, then the answer is yes.

In June of 2010 I received a phone call explaining that even though my work and results were at an all-time high, because our NHL team did not advance further than expected in the Stanley Cup Playoffs, CHANGE was going to happen. As an assistant coach on this team, apparently I was part of it. The next day I was scheduled to have my left hip replaced - talk about a devastating week!

Only a few times in my life have I wondered "why me?" and this was one of them. Had I experienced a bad season as an NHL coach then I could understand getting fired, but everything that I was asked to do that season was the best in team history. We went from not making the playoffs the year before I was hired, to winning our division for the 2 seasons I was there. In my more specific areas of responsibility, during my tenure the power play went from 18th best in the league to 6th best, face-offs improved from 24th in the league to 7th, and in offence, we went from 22nd in the NHL to second overall, with the league's MVP and scoring race winner.

Let's be frank with each other; I wasn't happy. The team of people I trusted had blind-sided me, and the Oxycontin I was given after my hip surgery dulled the physical pain, but did nothing to help my emotional disappointment. In a few words, for a few days, I was angry. I was losing a dream, and for the first time in many years, I was slowly losing my drive, my *hungry spirit*.

Sure, this is natural. We need time and space to get over the shock and pain, but WOW, isn't it amazing how a few words over the phone can instantly change our emotions, mindset and life-direction? So, here is the bad news and the great news wrapped in one: **just as a few words can dramatically change the direction of our lives in a negative way, so also a few inspiring ideas can dramatically change our lives for the better!**

I'm not going to pretend that I woke up the next day full of energy and ready to conquer the world. It did take time, but what I discovered during that time is that there is a process to re-fuelling our *hungry spirit*. Becoming *hungry* is the foundation to everything that we desire to do and be throughout our lifetime. Staying *hungry* will not only become our greatest challenge, but ultimately delivers our greatest success.

If we are not hungry we have little chance to play our *Best Game*!

At the time of writing, I am one of only 258 players to have played more than 1000 games in the National Hockey League. During my journey towards accomplishing this, something began to catch my attention. Many players that I competed against had more natural talent than I did, but they still dropped off or never made it to the next level. These players had all of the externally polished skills, but something was missing. It was the desire to compete, to improve, and to take the next important steps. In other words, for whatever reason, their *hungry* spirit was lagging.

Over my many years in both professional sport and business I have discovered that people who stay *hungry* have found a pattern, a process, or some important ingredients that allow their inner game to stay fuelled even when their outer game sputters. I am not attempting to create a psychological discourse on why people get depressed or excited here. Instead, I want to guide you on the pathway to generating exceptional performance.

The world of professional sport is my background, but I spend as much time now with CEO's, Presidents, and Managers – players at the corporate and organizational level. Over the past 20 years

> "The rung of a ladder was never meant to rest upon, but only to hold a man's foot long enough to enable him to put the other somewhat higher."
>
> **Thomas Huxley**

of weaving in and out between sports and business, the realization has been reinforced again and again to me that the principles that create success, high performance, team development and exemplary leadership are always the same.

The first principle that struck me to be true across culture, vocation, generation and gender is that "what we focus on, we get." People who stay *hungry* have a heightened focus with a successful Game Plan. With or without intention, our life is shaped as we play out the 3 key components of our Game Plan: our Inner Game, our Outer Game, and our Team Game.

The Inner Game is the core process which enables our *hungry spirit* to thrive. Like everything else in life, the *hungry spirit* runs on fuel. Just as cars run on gas or electricity, and our bodies run efficiently on nutritious food, our lives are energized by certain ingredients. The Inner Game runs on 3 types of core fuel: Purpose & Passion, Futuring, and Believing.

The Outer Game, by contrast, focuses on performance and execution. We take our inner energy to the world around us. The Outer Game runs on 3 types of performance fuel: Framing, Constructing, and Rebounding.

Finally, none of us live isolated lives. We all play on teams: corporate teams, family teams, cultural teams, political teams, and yes, sports teams. The way we do team influences, and is influenced by, our *hungry spirit*. The Team Game runs on 3 types of relational fuel: Deflecting, Honouring, and Connecting.

Introducing the Hungry Spirit

I have lived for just over one-half century, watching and working with many of the most successful and highest performing people in the world. Over the last 30 years I have observed a second principle common to both high performers and excellent leaders: they are never satisfied with the status quo! *Leaders are Learners*; they never stop trying to improve. To do this, they begin by asking great questions. The best in the world tend to ask pointed questions which focus their action, and give them superior insights. With that in mind, here are some questions that

I have been asking around *hungry*:

- What is the difference between people who maximize their abilities/opportunities and those who don't?
- Why are some people with less talent and less education, more successful?
- What drives people to be their very best?
- How can people love what they do and be good at it too?
- What is the spark that fuels people to be the best of the best?
- Why do some people conquer difficulty and disease when their circumstances suggest that they can't?

Success is complicated and achieving it is different for each of us. For that reason, I will not offer one specific solution that, when applied like an aspirin, will ease life's pain and guarantee riches. You won't find any "how-to" actions that falsely guarantee broad success here, but you will become much better acquainted with the common inner energy that initiates and fuels all successful action.

> "Our greatest enemies, the ones we must fight most often, are within."
>
> **Thomas Paine**

As life advances, the best in the world advance their perspective along with it. Mark Twain did: "When I was fourteen years old, my father was so ignorant I hated to have the old man around. But when I was twenty-one, I was surprised to see how much he had learned in only seven years." As our life advances, intrinsic motivators become more important. Emily Dickinson wrote, "Things may happen around you, and things may happen to you, but the only things that really count are the things that happen in you." It is time to focus on a newer perspective. It is time to upgrade the software that drives your human hardware. It is time to fire up your *hungry spirit*.

Let me tell you what I am *hungry* to accomplish right here. I deeply desire this book to be about you, and that reading it will inspire an atmosphere within you that stimulates decisive change! Every person alive today is *hungry* to some degree and on some level. Whether your *hungry spirit* is immature, injured or incomplete, or fuelled-up and firing on all cylinders, my hope is that the following pages will inspire your inner game, your outer game and your team game, igniting your *hungry spirit* to its highest level. It's your journey! Robert Louis Stevenson said, "Don't judge each day by the harvest you reap, but by the seeds you plant." Planting the seeds of internal change today creates tomorrow's harvest. It's your *hungry spirit* to fuel, feed and protect–yours first, and then your team's. And as you do, you will increase your impact on a world in desperate need of your Best Game!

> "If you deliberately plan to be less than you are capable of being, then I warn you that you will be deeply unhappy for the rest of your life. You will be evading your own capacities, your own possibilities"
>
> **Abraham Maslow**

[signature]

Ryan Walter

Player, Coach, Speaker, Transformational Leader
A guy just like you, who deeply desires to stay HUNGRY!

1

The
Hungry Spirit

!

HUNGRY

When the Hungry Spirit is Damaged

I was in a typical twenty-first century rush. Our pool looked a
lot more like something Popeye would eat than a place he would
cool off with Olive Oyl, and I desperately needed to shock the
water back to some semblance of clear. So with a hundred other
things to do in my day, I ran into aisle 34 of my favourite big box
store where I had purchased pool items in the past. There, almost
at the very end, was the pool shock that I needed. I lifted the
largest container and at that moment remembered that we needed
one other pool item. Scrambling and searching unsuccessfully
for it, I finally resorted (it's a guy thing not to ask first) to finding
someone who could help me. I hauled my heavy container of
pool shock up the aisle, found a woman wearing the special big

box store shirt and addressed her politely: "Excuse me, Ma'am; I am in a real rush. Could you help me find this particular pool item?" Without even looking up she snapped out, "Everything pool is in aisle 34," and continued what she was doing.

A funny thing happened in that moment as I stood there, stunned by her ambivalent attitude. I must be getting old and crotchety because for the first time in my life I decided that even though this had always been my favourite big box store, I would exercise my purchasing options! In that moment I decided never to shop at that particular store again. For some weird reason, I did the math at home, later that evening. The "everything pool is in aisle 34" woman didn't lose a mere $79.95 sale; she lost a $79,000.00 lifetime customer!

This woman was a mature worker. She knew the ropes and the consequences. She was off her game and because of her attitude, her team paid a huge price. My pro-sports background suggests to me that the "everything pool is in aisle 34" woman was either disillusioned with her team (a culture in need of attention), turned off by an ineffective leader (people don't leave companies; they leave people), or living with an uninspired Inner Game. Her *hungry spirit* was nonexistent or at best, had slowed to a crawl. Unfortunately, she is not alone. Seventy-five percent of people responding to a recent Forbes poll claimed to be "unfulfilled" and "unhappy" with their jobs, while roughly 30 percent were outright negative: "I hate my job... if it weren't for the pay-check, I'd leave tomorrow." What a sad statement... what a human tragedy.

Understanding Hungry

Few of us would deny that physical hunger is a major problem in our world. While millions of people over-eat, the knowledge that many more millions go to bed hungry each evening is a travesty.

The ironic dichotomy is that as the stomach aches for food, so also the human heart aches for significance. As food fuels our physical energy, our *hungry* spirit drives us toward greater significance. Both are essential for real life!

> "The difference between what we are doing and what we're capable of doing would solve most of the world's problems."
>
> **Mahatma Gandhi**

I believe that every team, organization and company shares two basic qualities. They have a SMART side and they have a HEART side.

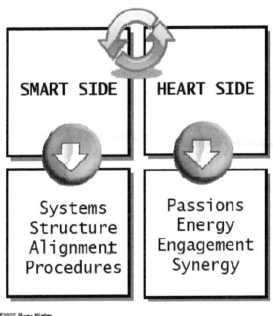

™2007 Ryan Walter

Individuals and organizations demonstrate that they are *smart* in the way they plan, organize, improvise, devise strategy, create structure and systematize what they desire to accomplish. Individuals and organizations demonstrate their *heart* through their passion to achieve, their personal and cultural energy, their constant focus on purpose, and their attention to the cultural heartbeat. Both the *smart side* and the *heart side* must be aligned for sustained success. It is essential to ignite the emotional energy that resides in the *heart side* of people and cultures so the *smart side* can flourish.

Some leaders poo-poo spending money on what they call the soft qualities of life, business and sport. They say, "I pay them to work... they should motivate themselves." Remember, however, that the "everything pool is in aisle 34" woman was on top of the *smart side* of her job. The store aisles were stocked. The cashiers were ready to take my money. So why didn't I buy? Because on the *heart side*, the inner enthusiasm of the "everything pool is in aisle 34" woman was damaged.

> "Without a compelling cause, our employees are just putting in time. Their minds might be engaged, but their hearts are not. Meaning precedes motivation."
>
> **Lee J. Colan**

The Hungry Spirit is Culturally Connected

I feel very fortunate to have played for 3 NHL teams. Playing professional hockey was my dream while I was growing up and I cherished every practice, game, goal, win, and even every broken bone. During my final NHL season I dressed for only 22 of 82 games for the Vancouver Canucks, so on my last visit to New York's famed Madison Square Garden as a player, I was relegated to watching from the press box. This was, in fact, my first time visiting the press box in Madison Square. In today's antiseptic new mega-buildings the press box is often far from the reach or touch of the paying public, but in that game I soon came to appreciate that the last row of seats actually butts-up to the first row of the press box.

The game was progressing nicely from the Canucks' point of view as Referee Kerry Fraser had just called 4 straight penalties against the home-town Rangers. As you can imagine, the Garden's faithful didn't particularly like the actions of the referee, especially after my team scored on the power play. I had experienced the "Bronx Cheer" from ice-level many times but never at arm's length. The Ranger fans rose with anger and, as with one voice, began to chant, "FRASER SUCKS," FRASER SUCKS," "FRASER SUCKS."

Concealing an under-my-breath snicker I began to watch the four people directly in front of me. From what I could glean, three buddies in their early 40's were sitting together, and the fellow on the left had brought along what I judged to be his 12 year old son. As the Ranger fans started to really get into the "Bronx Cheer" for referee Fraser, I became fascinated by the dynamic happening right in front of me. The three buddies joined the cheer: "FRASER SUCKS," FRASER SUCKSS," "FRASER SUCKSSS." The young boy sat quietly, watching his Dad's actions intently. As the chant accelerated into a full chorus, I wondered what was going through the mind of the young fan in front of me. All of a sudden, with great enthu-siasm and excitement, the young boy jumped up and shouted in unison with his Dad, "FRASER SUCKSSS," "FRASER SUCKSSSS!"

> "Nothing so conclusively proves a man's ability to lead others as what he does day to day to lead himself."
> **Thomas Watson Sr.**

What happened next was devastating to the young boy and frus-trating to me. The man grabbed his son, looked him directly in the eye, wagged his index finger at him and yelled, "No, not you. Sit down," and then turned to rejoin the chorus of "FRASER SUCKSSSSS!"

Ouch! In that instant I saw the crushed *hungry* spirit drain from the little boy's heart. His excitement disappeared. His personal enthusiasm dampened. His shoulders slouched, and he sat there, his inner game visibly shattered from the hurtful words which had been spewed in his direction from someone obviously close to him.

Something pinged in my own heart that night. I really felt for that young boy! What we do and say directly impacts the *hungry spirit* of those we lead.

We are interdependent people who feed off the energy of both our leaders and the people around us. Feeding the *hungry* spirit is our personal responsibility, but our *hungry* spirit is also influenced positively and negatively by our leaders, and interdependently fuelled or deflated in the context of our teams, including families, friends, and work units.

Come on boys, get HUNGRY!

> "Let me tell you the secret that has led me to my goal. My strength lies solely in my tenacity."
> **Louis Pasteur**

How many hundreds of times have I heard that shouted across countless NHL dressing rooms? When I played in the NHL, the *hungry* concept was referenced continually, especially in the playoffs, when every-thing was on the line. "Come on boys, we're not HUNGRY enough!" would resonate throughout the hallway as our team walked off the ice after a lacklustre period of play. Our team's deep desire to forge on towards the Stanley Cup finals increased our need for intensity and heightened our desire to muster more will. We all understood this *hungry* thing intuitively. In our minds it was about getting each other to the next level, increasing our desire to compete, and somehow finding a way to win. It had nothing to do with systems, yet everything to do with performance. It had nothing to do with team execution and yet everything to do with the emotional commitment and will to play hard that drives performance.

During the 1985-86 NHL season I played on an above average Montreal Canadiens team. Our team had its ups and downs but began to gain momentum during the '86 playoff run. We beat Boston in 3 games, Hartford in overtime in game 7, swept through New York on the back of a hot rookie goalie by the name of Patrick Roy, and finally met the Calgary Flames in the Stanley Cup finals.

In 1986 our team's common heartbeat, articulated in the dressing room before game 5 by my teammate Bobby Smith, was simply, "Boys we better do it now; most of us may never get this chance again." Independent of what motivated us we had created an intense cultural *hungry spirit*. In 1986 we won the Stanley Cup, beating Calgary in that game 5.

The next time we met Calgary in the finals, at the culmination of the 1989 Cup run, our team was up 2 games to 1 heading into game 4. I cannot begin to describe the personal elation I felt prior to that game, having experienced the thrill of scoring the game-winning, double-overtime goal in Game 3 two nights earlier. At this point, if our team could win game 4, we would go up 3 games to 1 in the best of 7 series, and the odds of winning a second Stanley Cup would increase twentyfold. During game 4 I was checked into Mike Vernon, the Flames' star goalie, and as I got up, Verny took a swipe at me with his blocker. In the heat of that battle I said some

> "Don't ever forget that you play with your soul as well as your body."
> **Kareem Abdul-Jabbar**

words that I have always regretted: "Verny, you're a loser and you're going to lose again!" What happened next was incredibly revealing. The fire, the will, the *hungry spirit* that I saw in Mike

Vernon's eyes that night should have warned me that we were in trouble. The Flames won game 4 and game 5, and finally won the Stanley Cup in game 6.

The difference between winning and losing very often comes down to the internal energy of will, desire and commitment. In 1986 we wanted that Cup so badly we could taste it. In 1989 we wanted it badly too, but the Flames were *hungrier.*

Winston Churchill understood the importance of his nation's will, desire, and commitment. Facing annihilation, I believe that Churchill purposed to ignite Britain's *hungry spirit* when he spoke these famous words: "We shall go on to the end, we shall fight on the seas and oceans, we shall fight with growing confidence and growing strength in the air, we shall defend our Island, whatever the cost may be, we shall fight on the beaches, we shall fight on the landing grounds, we shall fight in the fields and in the streets, we shall fight in the hills; we shall never surrender." From the NHL to the beaches of Britain to the corporate arena, staying and playing *hungry* is essential for success.

Who is Hungry?

Author Evan Thomas said of Bobby Kennedy in *Robert Kennedy--His Life*, "He was not a very good organizer, he was not good at follow-through, and he was not always realistic... he would say, 'Let's have a tea for 500 people tomorrow in Worcester Mass.' Kennedy's failings as an organizer, his impatience, his amateurism, his predilection for going outside the channels - would become problematic. But his shortcomings were hidden by the sheer force of his determination." Bobby Kennedy's determination was evidence of the relentless hunger displayed throughout his tragically-shortened life. You have to admit, if there is one word that describes the entire Kennedy clan, it is *hungry.*

Pause here and list 3 people in your life who you recognize to be *hungry*:

1._____

2._____

3._____

Think about the transferable qualities in the people you have identified and keep those qualities on the periphery of your mind as you journey deeper.

Information vs. Inspiration

In today's age of CNN and news headlines by text, I believe there is a huge gulf between *information* and *inspiration*. Most information comes as a statement, but never contains an example to follow or concludes with a solution. Let me show you what I mean.

The photo below is a small river (or creek) near our home. Every day my family and I drive by and over this Little Campbell River.

One day little signs began to pop up:

Every day our family would drive by the river and read the signs.

And then one day my wife, Jenn and I, laughed and laughed at a new sign that appeared:

Someone who drove by these signs daily (just like us) must have become frustrated (just like us). But, they did something about it. They put up the sign which asked, "HOW?" People often disseminate information (Save the Little Campbell) but never tell us why or show us how.

Statements and Solutions

We receive statements and information daily, but most of us suffer underlying frustration because these statements seldom offer a solution. During my years as a professional athlete I had many coaches who could tell us what was wrong with our skills or tactics, but few coaches had the wisdom to help us create a solution that would inspire our forward movement. The best transformational leaders create inspiration by closing the gap between statement and solution. As you apply the *hungry* process you can bridge this gap and inspire the next season of your life.

Where can we buy a *Hungry Spirit?*

People travel vast distances and squander vast sums of money with the hopes of becoming rich or significant when, in fact, the potential for attaining both is waiting within. Thousands of people left everything behind and endured incredible hardships in the California Gold Rush of 1848. Precious few discovered any gold at all, and the real tragedy is that they missed Missouri's zinc, Oklahoma's oil, Kansas's wheat, and Utah and Nevada's uranium along the way. We flock to get rich quick schemes, or internet scams, when spending comparable time and energy digging deeper to uncover our Purpose and Passion would yield vastly greater odds of accomplishing our dreams. I'll give you some good news: racheting up your *hungry spirit* doesn't take a trip to the Gold Rush. It begins with your Inner Game.

Just before you open the map to the Inner Game in Section I, let me take you on a detour to Washington, DC where I joined 200 executives at the Willard Hotel. My keynote focussed on Leading

Hungry Teams. I started my professional hockey career with the Washington Capitals from 1978 to 1982, so it was amazing for my wife and me to return to see the core of the city again.

We discovered one significant change in the National Mall: the addition of the WW II Memorial between the Lincoln and Jefferson Memorials. As we walked the periphery, the words of Walter Lord etched into the east wall, jumped out at me:

"They had no right to win, yet they did and in doing so they changed the war... Even against the greatest of odds there is something in the human spirit, a magic blend of skill, faith and valour that can lift men from certain defeat to incredible victory."

Walter Lord was describing the inner qualities that produced outward victory at the Battle of Midway June 4-7, 1942. Then and now, fuelling the *hungry spirit* begins with the Inner Game.

INNER GAME

CORE FUEL

Purpose & Passion

Futuring

Believing

Chapter

Hungry Core:

Purpose & Passion

HUNGRY

Get back to the CORE

The words *hungry spirit* sound spiritual, and that is exactly the point. People who consistently live a *hungry* life are in touch with their hearts. Martin Luther King Jr. understood that the root cause of society's problems was spiritual: "Our scientific power has outrun our spiritual power, **we have guided missiles and misguided men!**" He also stated, "If a man hasn't discovered something that he will die for, he isn't fit to live." Here is what happens when we lose touch with the *heart side* of life.

Early in my NHL career and early in our marriage, Jenn needed to apply for her US resident alien status or green card. We were both Canadian, and even though I already had my green card, the process was still relatively new to both of us. Since I was playing for the Washington Capitals at the time and our residence was just outside of Washington DC, we went to the nearest immigration office in downtown Baltimore.

> "Whenever there was an opportunity for it, one had to give them a why - an aim - for their lives, in order to strengthen them to bear the terrible how of their existence. Woe to him who saw no more sense in his life, no aim, no purpose, and therefore no point in carrying on. He was soon lost."
>
> **Victor Frankl**

We arrived together and settled into a long line and a longer wait. Hours went by before my wife's name was finally called. We walked into a normal office with a seemingly normal immigration officer behind the desk, but that was as much normal as we were going to get. Without looking up, the officer stared through his reading glasses at Jenni's file and started our meeting by looking at his watch and stating precisely how many days, hours and minutes of work he had left before his retirement. We sat in shocked silence, broken only by nervous laughter on our part, to which we were admonished, "Don't laugh," a phrase which would be uttered repeatedly by our officer in response to statements we were sure had to be jokes, but apparently were not.

> "If you can't work with joy, you should leave your work and go sit at the gate of the temple and beg for alms from those who can."
>
> **Kahlil Gibran**

The officer's hard eyes then bored a hole through Jenn as he asked her, "Have you ever been smuggled into the United States of America in the trunk of a car?" My heart was pumping adrenaline at this point and I was rapidly entering "defending my wife" mode. Jenn, flustered, answered, "No, never." And then he pulled out the big intimidation stick... and asked my young bride, "At any point in your life have you ever been a prostitute?" My stunned wife slumped and scowled. Meanwhile, full of anger, I was practically readying to go over the top rope. This disenchanted man hated his job and made it his mission in life to reduce as many people as possible down to his energy level. I pointed out earlier that the *hungry spirit* is personal but interdependent and this story is a great example. As a young couple we experienced feelings of collective anger, disappointment and embarrassment, all because of one person's decision to wallow in his self-made cesspool instead of discovering his Purpose and Passion and focusing on these to add value to humanity.

An easy indicator of whether you are living firmly in your Purpose and Passion is revealed by answering this simple question: **What kind of energy generation station are you?** Are you a *user* or a *source*, or in other words, do you suck or supply energy? Our immigration official was stuck working with no sense of winning. People living their Purpose and Passion generate energy and add value to humanity. They are living, working, and doing what they were built to do. They are supplying positive vibes because to them life is so much more than a garbage dump full of people to climb over; it has meaning.

Tragically, the green card man ruined more than other people's days, he also ruined his own. By failing to pursue his very best for his highest purpose, like a death-eater gone wrong, he inadvertently sucked the life out of his own soul. Mankind, whether in the service of government, processing green cards, or as articulated by Victor Frankl from inside a German prison camp, must have a passion-filled purpose, or the essence of life will be lost.

> "You can use most any measure when you're speaking of success. You can measure it in fancy home, expensive car, or dress. But the measure of your real success is one that you cannot spend—it is the way your child describes you when talking to a friend."
> **Martin Baxbaum**

Englishman Thomas Parr lived from 1483 to 1635. His 152 year-long life was the source for the expression, "are you feeling up to par?" whose words describe feeling dynamically alive.

Let's explore together how to increase our ability to stay dynamically alive.

As I completed my Master of Arts in Leadership/Business at age 47, it struck me how often the core principles behind my studies of leadership, high-performance and team always connected initially around the concepts of Purpose and Passion. According to comedian Dave Gardner: "Success is getting what you want; happiness is wanting what you get." John Maxwell goes a little deeper: "**Success is... knowing your purpose in life, growing to reach your maximum potential, and sowing the seeds that benefit others.**" I believe that true success is directly connected to finding and following your life's purpose.

PURPOSE

Professional baseball player, preacher, and orator, Billy Sunday said that, "more men fail through lack of purpose than lack of talent." According to Helen Keller, "Many persons have a wrong idea of what constitutes real happiness. It is not obtained through self-gratification, but through fidelity to a worthy purpose." The Sufi poet Rumi tells us to think of our lives as if we had been sent by a king to a distant country with a special task. All of us are on a quest to make a life for ourselves that is purposeful. "You might do a hundred other things, but if you fail to do the one thing for which you were sent it will be as if you had done nothing." To sustain the *hungry spirit* we must find our place of personal purpose.

I have asked my hundreds of clients and thousands of participants, while conducting two hour to two day leadership development sessions, "What is purpose?" A slight pause usually fills the room and then the same four or five suggestions tend to be offered: "it's a goal, a mission, a desired direction, the reason we do what we do."

The dictionary definition of purpose:

1. the reason for which something exists or is done, made, used, etc.
2. an intended or desired result; end; aim; goal.
3. the subject in hand; the point at issue.
4. practical result, effect, or advantage: *to act to good purpose.*
5. to set an aim, intention, or goal for oneself.
6. to resolve (to do something): *He purposed to change his way of life radically.*

The Bible explains that mankind is born with and for a purpose. I love studying famous people, trying to understand how and why they made a difference in the course of history. David, in the Old Testament is one of those people. Saul, the king of Israel had a whole army full of soldiers who could have challenged Goliath. Why then was only David brave enough to do

> "Everyone has a special purpose, a special talent or gift to give others, and it's your duty to discover what it is. Your special talent is God's gift to you. What you do with your talent is your gift to God."
> **Gautama Chopra**

it? Later, when Saul was rejected as King of Israel, the prophet Samuel explains what it was about David that made such a difference: "But the Lord said to Samuel about David's brother, "Don't be impressed by his appearance or his height, for I have rejected him. God does not view things the way men do. People look on the outward appearance, but the Lord looks at the heart." (Samuel 16:7) God then chose David to be the next King of Israel. Outer success originates inside the heart.

In his 1946 book, *Man's Search for Meaning,* Victor Frankl describes how he discovered that the meaning

> "Having a why—a powerful, compelling reason—is the one thing no one can give you."
> **Stephan Pierce**

of life is found in every moment of living, even when that life was lived in a Nazi concentration camp. Frankl observed that a prisoner's psychological reactions are not solely the result of his imprisonment, but are also determined by the freedom of choice he always has, even in the midst of severe suffering. It is only when a prisoner loses faith in the future that he is doomed. "We who lived in concentration camps can remember the men who walked through the huts comforting others, giving away their last piece of bread. They may have been few in number, but they offer sufficient proof that everything can be taken from a man but one thing: the last of the human freedoms—to choose one's attitude in any given set of circumstances, to choose one's own way."

Nietzsche's words, **"He who has a why to live for can bear with almost any *how*"** contributes an additional thought to this discussion. "The opposite of courage in our society is not cowardice… it is conformity." It is not enough to discover your purpose; you must develop the courage to live by it. Conforming to the throng of people standing next to you is the norm, but I am asking you to discover the specific why for your life that allows you to bear any *how*. Our immigration officer did not have the courage to leave a job he hated in order to discover and pursue his true purpose. Personal purpose distinguishes each of us from every other person in this world.

> "Courage is resistance to fear, mastery of fear -- not absence of fear."
>
> **Mark Twain**

When the alarm goes off on Monday morning, what can't you wait to *get going on*?

1.
2.
3.
4.

Do you see a theme emerging that could be your purpose?

_____

_____

What would you do if you won 4 million dollars in a lottery and learned the same day that you only had 4 months to live? Who would you spend time with? How would you spend your money? Who would you apologize to?

_____

_____

_____

_____

PASSION

Passion is different from, although related to purpose. Keith Ferrazzi says in *Never Eat Alone*, "A passion is how you choose to live your life. A goal [purpose] is something you aim to achieve."

Passion is described as:

1. any powerful or compelling emotion or feeling, as love or hate.
2. strong amorous feeling or desire; love; ardor.
3. a strong or extravagant fondness, enthusiasm, or desire for anything: a passion for music.
4. the object of such a fondness or desire: *Accuracy became a passion with him.*
5. an outburst of strong emotion or feeling: *He suddenly broke into a passion of bitter words.*
6. the state of being acted upon or affected by something external, esp. something alien to one's nature or one's customary behaviour.

Where Purpose is logical, Passion is emotional. It extends to all areas of our lives, but can be fleeting. Pittsburgh Penguins Captain and NHL MVP Sydney Crosby told me: "You find ways to channel your emotion. For some guys it's easier than others. For my game, I need to be emotional. When the energy's not there, when the passion is gone, I don't think that I'll ever be the same player. The passion and emotion have to be there. It's a matter of channelling it, and I'm still learning how to do that. Just because you get to the NHL doesn't mean that you stop learning. For some guys that's easier than for others. I believe that I have to play with a bit of an edge, and that just comes from wanting to compete and wanting the puck and wanting to be involved."

Passion ignites both positive and negative energy, but life lived without it hardly seems worth living. One of Japan's leading entrepreneurs, Kazuo Inamori, says, "Your passion is the source of success and accomplishment; the stronger your will, enthusiasm and passion for success, the better your chance to succeed."

List the most recent times you remember being passionate, what you became passionate about, and why.

	When?	What?	Why?
1.			
2.			
3.			
4.			

An Important Reminder

Purpose and Passion very seldom identify themselves in one specific occupation. These two powerful forces in our lives give direction to what we should do, but they are more about how we do what we do. I was passionate about playing NHL hockey and felt that it was well within my purpose. But let's go deeper. Why was I built to do what I was doing? In retrospect I can now see that it was the components of the game that I adored. I was attracted to the competition, team atmosphere and leadership challenges of winning. I can also play these aspects of my combined Purpose and Passion out in a number of other occupational arenas. This is probably why some professional athletes go on to be successful business people: they transfer the elements of their Purpose and Passion from their sport to compete in business.

Over the course of my lifetime I am thankful to never have been in prison, but very thankful to have met many people on the inside of prisons. My work with the Justice Institute of British Columbia, encouraging and inspiring their Correctional Officers through Leadership/Team Regeneration Sessions, gave me the opportunity to once again visit men in custody. Visiting "inside" had never bothered me before, but during my last opportunity with officers and prisoners, my visit to the storage centre for confiscated criminal contraband really upset me.

I was impressed by the incredible creativity of the prisoners who had fashioned the contraband. Many of these people spent their living hours "inside," passionate about creating knuckle-busters out of plastic chairs, knives out of tooth brushes, and switchblades out of pieces of plates and table tops. I soon became angry and frustrated thinking about the way these prisoners were maximizing the use of their time and utilizing their talent … but to what end? My heart ached as I imagined how these people could benefit from using their creativity for good. They could be supplying instead of sucking energy, adding value to society instead of finding ways to take away life.

In the words of Eric Butterworth: "When we do less than our best, or use our best for less than our best purposes, we cheat ourselves." It's not enough to be our best or to beat our best. Being our best for the best, pure purposes of our life

> "You can only become truly accomplished at something you love. Don't make money your goal. Instead, pursue the things you love doing, and then do them so well that people can't take their eyes off of you."
>
> **Maya Angelou**

is the key to personal fulfilment and staying *hungry*. When we don't bring our very best to the table we often sense that we have cheated our teammates, friends or family, but we seldom see *less than our very best* as cheating ourselves.

I am not so naive as to think that all of these prisoners will rehabilitate and add value to society, but some do. The incarcerated inmates who do seem to turn the corner and come out of this brutal environment changed and ready to contribute to society all have one common trait. They have found their Inner Game, a new Purpose and Passion, and have re-ignited their *hungry spirit*. The 21st century is not in need of people leading mediocre lives. Today's world demands our best and is continuously searching for people who actualize their Purpose and Passion. Purpose and Passion move us away from what we have to do–towards what we want to do and should be doing. They are the inner fuel supply of a *hungry spirit*.

The Hungry Quadrant

Any desired change always starts with understanding our current reality. We can't know where to go if we don't know where we are. Understanding what *hungry* is, often comes directly from a better understanding of what *hungry* isn't. In the *Hungry Quadrant* below, Purpose is placed on the north/south axis and Passion on the east/west axis. The 4 zones, which follow, describe the 4 states that result from differing levels of Purpose and Passion.

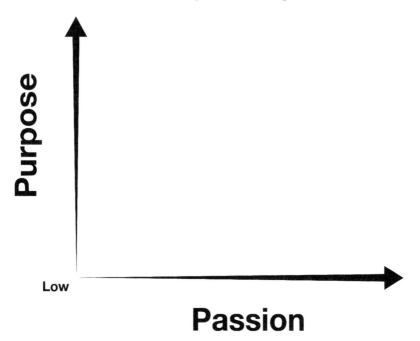

Low Purpose - Low Passion

The bottom of Purpose and the bottom of Passion is the low of low, a place we seldom desire to be either personally or culturally. Purposeless living breeds lethargy. Living in the low purpose portion of the quadrant, long term, squelches both the spark and energy needed to fuel and sustain the *hungry spirit*. Since passion is emotional energy, you can imagine what a life low on passion looks like. The intersection of low purpose and low passion leaves people and teams stuck in a place that most despise. I call this the **Ambivalent** Zone.

The French/American writer and 1986 Nobel Peace prize winner, Elie Wiesel, has said:

"The opposite of love is not hate, it's indifference.
The opposite of art is not ugliness, it's indifference.
The opposite of faith, is not heresy, it's indifference.
And the opposite of life, is not death, it's indifference."

Let me add that the opposite of *hungry* is not *full*, it's ambivalence.

Many of my clients have offered the following descriptors for their practical understanding of what ambivalence feels like:

*   don't care
*   want out
*   not engaged
*   can't wait for it to be over
*   I'm stuck here–this is my lot in life.
*   who cares?
*   getting by
*   I don't care any more

As you now know, our Montreal Canadiens team landed back in the Stanley Cup final during the 1989 playoff run, ultimately losing to Calgary. I always find it humorous that in sport when you are an older team and you win, you are mature, but when you are an older team and you lose, you are *old*! The next season many of our older players, of which I was one, started to get downsized, or do they call it right-sized? When my coach at the time screamed at me, I felt it was unjustified and was disappointed that my teammates didn't seem to back me up. I found myself sitting on a Montreal Canadiens bench making hundreds of thousands of dollars, totally *ambivalent*. The prevalent thought in my mind was, "If they don't care… I don't care." How many Stanley Cups are you going to win with me or my teammates in that state? NONE! Fortunately, I used many of the ingredients highlighted in this book to quickly help myself out of the funk and back into a more *hungry* state.

If we are human, we find ourselves at the ambivalent crossroads of low Purpose and low Passion once in awhile, but the key to a dynamic life is to make this stop, a short stop. Ambivalence is an architected attitude that is unfortunately a permanent home for people who live a purposeless existence, upset with their so called "bad luck" in life. This state stems from the belief that other factors control our destiny and that other people don't possess nearly the bad fortune that we have encountered. People living in this zone have given away personal power only to become powerless. Albert Schwitzer, another Nobel Prize-winning French philosopher, believed **"the tragedy of life is what dies inside a person while they live."**

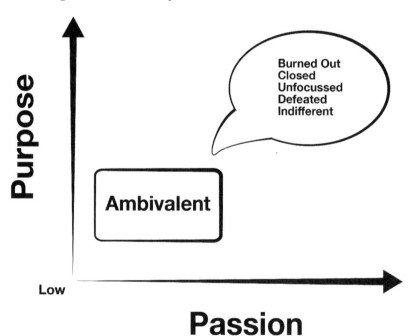

High Purpose - Low Passion

If we move up the north/south axis towards a place of high Purpose, but low Passion, we become **Frustrated**. We understand perfectly our purpose in life, but for whatever reason are unable to generate the energy, focus or gumption to get it done. A leader's frustration can boil over when his or her clear personal direction produces less than stellar results. When we know, personally and culturally, exactly what needs to be accomplished, but lack the emotional energy to get it done at a high level, we are stuck in the zone of frustration.

In my work, I have encountered many leaders who know exactly what their team should do (high Purpose), but for whatever reason are having trouble generating the team energy and synergy (low Passion) to make these things happen. A leader's first responsibility is to energize his or her inner passion in order to avoid spending all of their working time in this part of the quadrant.

Frustration also flows when we are affronted by change or are at the front end of a losing streak. Rosabeth Ross Kanter sent teams of researchers to explore why certain corporations, companies and teams find themselves on losing or winning streaks. In her book, *Confidence*, Kanter breaks these findings down to three important concepts: Collaboration, Accountability and Initiative. She says that these words themselves are neutral. It is how we *do* these words that creates the losing or winning streak. If you are a leader who knows exactly what your team's purpose and goals are, but are having trouble evoking the emotional passion from your people to accomplish them, look hard at these three concepts with a view to discovering:

1. Your process to hold people accountable.
2. Your people's cultural confidence to take initiative.
3. How collaboration manifests on your team.

The sporting world yearly spits out examples of teams and individuals with a common, clear purpose (usually achieving a championship win), but with disjointed effort and little passion generated towards this clear purpose. I believe that the gap between knowing and getting it done is an enlightened leader's ability to inspire the passion of the team!

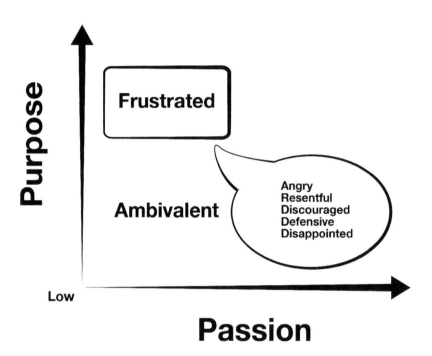

Low Purpose – High Passion

Move from low to high Passion on the east/west axis but also slide back down the north/south axis to the low Purpose zone. You have just entered the **Entertained** Zone. We tend to get excited here, but are not effective long term. I often found myself in this passionate place earlier in my life. My personality loves all of life; I have an explorative nature; I like new things and new ways of doing. I can easily slip in and out of the excited, but ineffective, entertained zone and have learned to continually ask myself the simple question: "Is this within the scope of my high Purpose?" This has been critical for keeping me *hungry* over the long haul.

The dictionary describes being entertained as being "pleasantly occupied." Entertained is just the word for this area of low Purpose and high emotional energy. It's a little like watching an average movie at a brand new theatre. Two and a half hours of excitement and entertainment, a little popcorn and we're on to something else. In the entertained society in which we live, the key to sustaining our *hungry spirit* is to stay passionate around what we were built to do--our purpose. I believe that the reason many have not found significance is due to the distraction of the Entertained Zone. Living here is fun for a while, but unsatisfying in the long term.

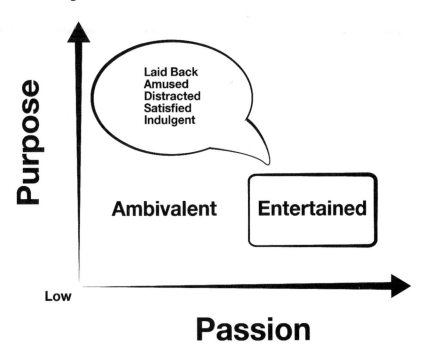

High Purpose – High Passion

When we are in the high Passion and high Purpose arena, we are **hungry**! We are living in the center of our gifting. Long-term living inside the *Hungry* Zone produces a sense of significance and fulfilment: "this is exactly what I was built to do!" Here Purpose and Passion heat up and melt together like two cheeses on a grilled sandwich. The *hungry* place is the *sweet* spot. Our hunger is sustainable. Our hunger generates our best energy. Our hunger increases our will to battle overwhelming obstacles. Staying *hungry* must become the priority of our lives.

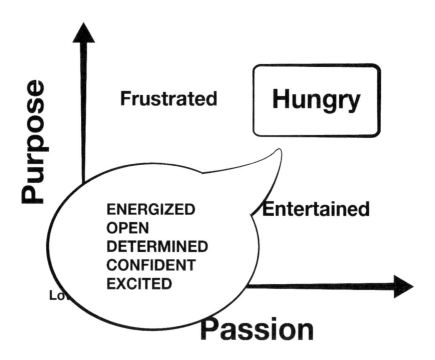

Along with co-author Mike Johnston, I asked high performing athletes from around the world what being *hungry* meant to them in *Simply the Best: Players on Performance*. NHL star forward Jarome Iginla answered: "I think it's focus and determination.

We always want to be good, but when you're hungry, it's a whole other level of focus and determination. When I'm playing my best, it's hard when the goals aren't going in and when I want to score a goal for the team, but I really feel I'm playing my best when I'm driving and competing and not thinking about the outcome and just going. It's another level of focus and determination."

A variety of my clients have described a 10-out-of-10 *hungry* player as:

- Fun
- Excited
- Focused
- Proactive
- Energized
- On top
- Communicative
- Supportive
- Challenger of the status quo
- Listener
- Informed
- Open
- Synergistic
- Courageous
- Tribal
- Winner
- Motivated

Of course, describing the *hungry* spirit and making it happen are two totally different challenges. You learn to play and stay *hungry* by making your journeys outside of the *hungry* zone as short as possible. You must tighten your emotional swings and cycles in order to stay true to your high Purpose and Passion.

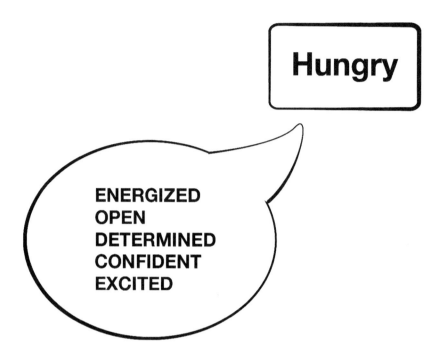

The *Hungry* indicators are words which perfectly describe the emotional state of players inside a Stanley Cup-winning dressing room. Make these emotions *your* personal and team's standard and you will be well on your way along the *hungry* journey. As the leader of yourself first and your team second, ponder whether you and your people can be described most often in these terms: energized, confident, open, determined, and excited?

Using a pen or pencil, shade in how full your **Purpose and Passion** tank is today. "How clear is your Purpose? How energized is your Passion?"

Your Personal and Team *Hungry* Exercise:

Look over the emotional indicators in the following diagram. In the blank boxes below them, place yourself and your people where they fit right now. The chapters that follow support your migration to, or continuation in, the *Hungry* Zone.

FRUSTRATED	HUNGRY
Angry Resentful Discouraged Defensive Disappointed	ENERGIZED OPEN DETERMINED CONFIDENT EXCITED
AMBIVALENT	**ENTERTAINED**
Burned Out Closed Unfocussed Defeated Indifferent	Laid Back Amused Distracted Satisfied Indulgent

FRUSTRATED	HUNGRY
AMBIVALENT	**ENTERTAINED**

Leadership Tips

1. Leaders have two broad ways to motivate their people: intrinsic and extrinsic motivators. Leaders wanting to develop their team's Best Game focus on understanding the Purpose and Passion of their players. Understanding why people want to do what they do reveals amazing opportunities for leaders to reward with intrinsic motivators.

2. The *Hungry Quadrant* not only gives us a snap shot of our personal *hungry spirit,* but also works well as a team indicator. I have played on teams where the leaders had no understanding of the temperature of the team and were surprised when everything fell apart. Use the Quadrant to better understand the indicators of where your team is now.

PURPOSE & PASSION
activates your HUNGRY CORE

Chapter

Hungry For:

Futuring

HUNGRY

Futuring

In the early 1950's Florence Chadwick became the first woman to swim the English Channel in both directions. On her first attempt she had been swimming for hours and was getting very near to the English coast. That's when the seas turned much colder and heavy swells developed. A dense fog settled in, blocking everything from view with a chilly, wet blanket. As Florence's pace slowed and energy drained, her mother called through the fog from one of the small boats following behind, "Come on, Florence, you can make it. It's only a little further." But she was exhausted and couldn't go on. As she slumped into the boat Florence felt defeated and was heart-broken when she realized how close she'd come. She later told the media, "I am not offering excuses, but I think that I could have made it if I had been able to **see my goal**."

On her next attempt, Florence developed a powerful mental image of the coast of England. She memorized every coastal feature and replayed those images again and again in her mind. This time she encountered the same discouraging conditions as before, but her **vision** saw her through to success. Charles Garfield says, "Peak performers, particularly in business, sports and the arts, report a highly developed ability to imprint images of successful actions in the mind. They practice mentally specific skills and behaviours leading to those outcomes and achievements which they ultimately attain."

The clearer and more specific our vision of what we are aiming for becomes, the more likely we are to accomplish it.

 I fly a lot. Since the age of 19, I have been spending much of my adult life in the air, between hockey road trips and now conferences, training sessions and client retreats. On one particular flight I was on the east coast of Canada flying to the Rocky Mountains to speak at a leadership conference.

The flight was departing at 7:30am eastern, I was well rested, I had my Starbucks coffee, and was sitting in an aisle seat. Just minutes before pulling away from the gate, a gentleman with a cap, and stars on his shoulders, asked if he could squeeze by me and take the middle seat. My disappointment in losing the extra elbow room soon turned to excitement as I realized that this was a commercial pilot sitting next to me, relocating to fly his next route!

What you may not know about me yet is that I have always

wanted to fly. I don't mean in the back of the plane, I mean in the cockpit. I have always wanted to fly my own little plane and now I had a professional pilot sitting next to me. What an amazing opportunity! I could ask him every question that I

> "Time flies. It's up to you to be the navigator."
> **Robert Orben**

ever wanted and he wouldn't be able to get away. By accident I poured coffee on him and we got to know each other. Just after take-off I turned to the pilot: "Mr. Pilot, I have always wanted to fly; could I ask you some questions?"

From the look on the pilot's face I sensed that he had been tortured like this before. Still, he graciously answered, "OK Ryan, go for it." I excitedly unloaded a rapid succession of questions and then launched into my next volley: "Mr. Pilot, Mr. Pilot, I have always wanted to know what you do on take-off if you puncture a wheel and the wing hits the ground and breaks off?"

At this point he'd had enough. The pilot turned to me and said, "Hold it, Ryan. If we are going to do this for the next four hours we may as well start at the beginning." The pilot took a deep breath and said, "**A pilot never takes off unless he or she has found a safe place to land.**"

I turned to the pilot and said, "Wow; that is so profound I need to think about it for the next four hours." Friends, this is the ingredient of Futuring.

> "In the absence of clearly-defined goals, we become strangely loyal to performing daily trivia until ultimately we become enslaved by it."
> **Robert Heinlein**

Where will you Land the Flights of Your Life?

I meet many people who live a life with no clear personal flight plan, and certainly no destination. After a short while the fuel gauge catches their eye and they see that it is nearly pointing to empty, so they simply put down at the first available landing strip. **If you do not have a strong sense of where you are going, it is impossible to stay *hungry*.**

It is never too late to reshape our tomorrow. We always have another chance to choose the landing strip of our desired destination. Where do you want to go? What do you want to accomplish? Who do you want to be? For some incredible reason, you were created to pursue and accomplish. Having a strong sense of what you would like your tomorrow to look like ignites your *hungry* energy and focuses it in that direction. NHL Stanley Cup winner, Scott Neidermayer said, "The number one way to get all players pulling together is to galvanize them around a strong vision of where we are going!"

> "Dream no small dreams, for they have no power to move the hearts of men. "
> **Johan Wolfgang Goethe**

Futuring: A Description

Futuring is the use of a systematic process for thinking about, and planning for the future. Futurists are people who actively view the present world as a window for possible future outcomes. They watch trends and try to envision what might happen. Futuring has its roots in the post–World War II era when scientists, politicians, and academics began to consider ways of anticipating the future. This initial consideration led to a more cohesive and developed field of Futuring in the mid-1960s.

I recently talked through the differences between leaders and managers with the vice-president of a large pulp and paper plant. Leadership is extremely important to his industry. The tremendous pressure from Indonesia and other parts of the world on the North American pulp industry has led to very competitive pricing per ton, forcing companies to do more with less. He told me he needs visionary leaders to give him energy and ideas. Before he does anything else he knows he must have clarity about the direction in which his business should go.

The first step toward benefitting from Futuring is to align our strengths, focus, and energy towards a specific destination. Dr. Ari Kiev, Associate Professor of Psychiatry, writes: "In my practice as a psychiatrist, I have found that helping people to develop personal goals has proven to be the most effective way to help them cope with problems. Observing the lives of people who have mastered adversity, I have noticed," he writes, "that they have established goals and sought with all their effort to achieve them. From the moment they decided to concentrate all their energies on a specific objective, they began to surmount the most difficult odds. The establishment of a goal is the key to successful living."

> "The greater danger for most of us lies not in setting our aim too high and falling short; but in setting our aim too low and achieving our mark."
> **Michelangelo**

The idea is to not only keep the vision in front of you, but to continuously drive towards increasing the clarity of your desired future. The clearer the vision, the more strongly you will move towards it. I have done this personally by actually drawing a picture of my goal. The visual nature of drawing a picture increases the imprint for me. With teams and companies I work with, I paper one wall of the room and starting on the left side, ask them to draw a detailed landscape of where they are today. Next, they draw on the right side, with as much visual vibrancy and colour as possible, where they would like to be. Finally, in the middle I ask them to record the action steps that are necessary to take them to their destination.

A second important step toward fully utilizing the ingredient of Futuring is to continuously make small adjustments along the way to maintain your *hungry spirit* momentum. Futuring is often like driving a car down a highway during the dark of night. You know your destination but the details of the road and landscape can only be viewed a little bit at a time, as your headlights reveal them. The good news is that as the driver of the car moves toward the curve, the lights of the car reach forward to illuminate the next bend.

To get the most out of the practice of Futuring, take action towards a goal and then practice small adaptations. As you start to move in the direction of fulfilling your vision, you will be required to take in new information and make smart, logical, iterative alignments. Pilots tell me that airplanes are off-course 90% of the time, and they must therefore continue to make small adjustments in order to land at their desired location.

Futuring is Plural

I find the plurality of Futuring to be invigorating! Some people have an overriding singular vision for their lives or their company, but most of us have many multiple directions that are small components of our overall vision. We need a vision for every part of our life not just one small compartment like business or sport. Our home life influences our working life which influences our health and the list goes on. As you activate Futuring in multiple areas, you will observe various facets of your life growing synergistically with a healthy, holistic *hungry spirit*.

"In 1989, college student Brian Scudamore encountered a tight summer job market in his hometown of Vancouver, Canada. So, after seeing an old, junk-hauling truck rumbling along a McDonald's drive-thru, he was inspired to start his own business. He named his junk removal service "The Rubbish Boys" and used the slogan: "We'll Stash Your Trash in a Flash!" What began as a means to pay for college quickly turned into a unique business – a franchise of professional junk removal.

> "Where there is no vision, the people perish,"
> **Proverbs 29:18**

Brian changed the company name to 1-800-GOT-JUNK?, invested in more trucks, hired great people, and set a goal to build a brand that would become a household name. Since 1998, the company has grown to approximately 200 locations across three countries."

I talked with Brian about the importance of Futuring to his business life. "Vision is everything," Brian told me, "but helping others see what you see is critical for making a business succeed." Brian has started what he calls a "Can you Imagine?" wall. His employees can place a dream, an idea, or a vision of what they want for the company on the wall and sign their name below. He then challenges them to find ways to make it happen.

Brian started the wall by writing: "Can you imagine 1-800-GOT-JUNK? being featured on the Oprah Winfrey show?" Months later both Brian and 1-800-GOT-JUNK? were center stage with Oprah. One person wrote, "Can you imagine operating our business in a third country?" Within a year 1-800-GOT-JUNK? opened in Australia. Another employee wrote, "Can you imagine being featured on a Starbucks Coffee cup?" Before long, Brian, 1-800-GOT-JUNK?, and his quote "You are what you can't let go of" were on the sleeve of Starbucks cups.

The "Can you Imagine?" wall helps people imagine what could be and, in a subliminal way, continuously energizes the *hungry* culture of Brian's company. Brian also continues to focus on possibilities. When the house that he was moving into required painting, Brian hired a company to paint the whole house in 24 hours. He loved the concept so much that he bought the company and is now launching WOW 1 Day Painting.

What can you imagine for your life?

_____

_____

_____

_____

_____

_____

_____

As you focus on your future, you will be pulled like a magnet towards what you want!

Futuring Starts with a Brain-Spark

Most Futuring starts with developing or brainstorming a simple idea.

Jeff Bezos's simple idea came from wondering what he could sell on the Internet and resulted in *Amazon.com*.

Reed Hastings's simple idea came from wondering why he was charged extra for a late video-return and resulted in *Netflix*.

Steve Jobs and Steve Wozniak's simple idea came from wondering why a computer had to be prohibitively expensive and take up an entire room and resulted in *Apple Computer*.

Fred Smith's simple idea to deliver packages overnight, resulted in *Federal Express*.

The distance between you and your desired Future is often only an idea away. It may be true that to be creative, you just need to have lots of ideas. If you have enough of them, they don't all have to be good. In this case, quantity is the road to quality. Or, you may have just one simple idea. Embrace it!

Futuring: The Process

In 1847 Charles Ellet Jr. was commissioned to build a bridge across the Niagara River. The 800 foot-wide Niagara Gorge was impossible to cross by boat because of Niagara Falls, so the cooperative American and Canadian Bridge Building companies came up with the idea of holding a kite-flying contest to extend a line across. A young American boy named Homan Walsh won the $5.00 prize by flying his kite from the Canadian side to the American side where it was fastened to a tree. A light cord was first attached to the kite string, then a heavier cord, then a rope and finally a 1,190 foot long wire cable, which was the beginning of the new suspension bridge.

From the single simple idea of holding a kite-flying contest, the first suspension bridge was constructed. The vision of Charles Ellet prompted ideas that sparked actions that created his desired reality. With a solid vision firmly in place, you and your people will get *hungry* towards accomplishing your desired future.

Futuring: People and Projects

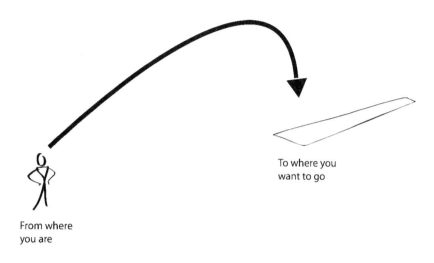

To where you
want to go

From where
you are

In their amazing book, *The Leadership Challenge,* James Kouzes and Barry Posner chronicle how they asked the following open-ended question to thousands of business and government executives over the past 25 years: "What values, personal traits, or characteristics do you look for and admire in a leader?" The two authors then reduced the resulting list of hundreds of answers and crafted it into a questionnaire titled "Characteristics of Admired Leaders." From this shorter list they asked people to select the four qualities that they "most look for and admire in a leader, someone whose direction they would willingly follow." The results have been consistent over the years and across cultures. Forward-looking was found to be the second most admired quality (behind honest) out of the top four Admired Leadership Characteristics.

> "Let us not seek to fix the blame for the past. Let us accept our own responsibility for the future."
>
> **John F. Kennedy**

1. Honest
2. **Forward-looking**
3. Inspiring
4. Competent

Across the teams I have been part of and observed in both sport and business, I have noticed that moving forward towards a desired goal or outcome reduces negative, complaining energy and enhances personal and cultural positive momentum. As you look to develop your leadership impact inside or outside of sport, business, or family, paying attention to forward-looking Futuring is

> "Dreams are renewable. No matter what our age or condition, there are still untapped possibilities within us and new beauty waiting to be born."
> **Dr. Dale E. Turner**

critical. The ingredient of Futuring stirs your *hungry spirit* to accomplish this enhanced future. Gallup's Marcus Buckingham tells us that "leadership is inspiring people to a better future." To actualize the better future we have to visualize the future better!

No doubt there is a dichotomy between creating your vision and then making it happen. It is important for you to slide your vision to what I call the peripheral. Know where you are going, but to borrow John Wooden's vernacular, focus now on "practicing the details that give you your vision." Futuring is essential for setting your direction, but once the direction is set, the critical component to reaching it is to focus on executing the plan. When I was part of the coaching staff on the NHL's Vancouver Canucks, we reminded each other not to continually focus on and talk about the desired outcome, but rather to stay focused on the process that would yield that outcome.

Futuring can be very practical. As Head Coach of the Canadian National Women's Team, Hockey Canada is just this week requesting my sports jacket size for the World Championships in

April. Coincidentally, I happen to be in the process of renewing my body size. Down 10 lbs already, with a goal of 10 more, I have requested that my jacket be tailored a size below my normal measurements. Making decisions today with our desired future in mind increases our ability to accomplish our goals.

> "So many of our dreams at first seem impossible, then they seem improbable, and then, when we summon the will, they soon become inevitable."
>
> **Christopher Reeve**

When he was young, Neil Armstrong, the astronaut, was playing in his back yard. His neighbours, Mr. and Mrs. Henry, were fighting again and he heard most of the conversation through one of their open windows. Mrs. Henry had just walked through her laundry list of things that she wanted Mr. Henry to change. After her volley, Mr. Henry decided to let his wife know some of his misgivings about the marriage. At the very end he spirited out, "and I want more sex." Mrs. Henry got very mad about this and while looking out their open window she shouted, "When that neighbour boy walks on the moon, you'll get more." After his retirement, Neil Armstrong, notorious for having walked on the moon, always ended every one of his countless speeches with, "Good luck, Mr. Henry!"

The cool thing about the future is that people do live their dreams, becoming astronauts, and doctors, and professional athletes. The more you *expect* your future to happen, the more it comes true. The ingredient of Futuring never fails to ignite your *hungry spirit*.

Using a pen or pencil, shade in how full your Futuring tank is today. How clear is the future you desire?

The Personal Futuring Exercise:

Goethe said: "Treat a man as he is and he will remain as he is. Treat a man as he can and should be, and he will become as he can and should be." Take the ingredient of Futuring and apply it to you and your people. Describe where you are today and then describe where you could be. Where would you like to land your plane?

Describe where you are today:

_____

_____

_____

_____

Describe where you will land your plane in the future:

_____

_____

_____

_____

Describe where you are with your family today:

_____

_____

_____

_____

Describe where you will land your family plane in the future:

_____

_____

_____

_____

Describe where your team is today:

_____

_____

_____

_____

Describe where you will land your team plane in the future:

_____

_____

_____

_____

Leadership Tips

1. Some leaders believe that vision is communicated once, and then everyone instantly gets moving towards making it happen. The great learning curve for leaders is to recognize that they must continually clarify and articulate the landing strip.

2. Make sure that you help each player on your team understand his or her part of the vision. Use the techniques of Futuring to help them better actualize their role. Clarity of shared vision increases your opportunity to have a *hungry* team.

Chapter

Hungry Heart:
Believing

We Get What We Believe

Our subconscious mind is neutral. Like a computer, it doesn't censure the information that we choose to load into it. Too often when we step up to the plate the images that fill our computer are negative and we then focus on what we can't do.

Baseball great Pete Rose was being interviewed during Spring Training the year he was about to break Ty Cobb's all time hits record. One reporter blurted out, "Pete, you only need 78 hits to break the record. How many at bats do you think that you'll need to get the 78 hits?"

Without hesitation, Pete just stared at the reporter and very matter-of-factly said, "78."

The reporter yelled back, "Ah, come on Pete, you don't expect to get 78 hits in 78 at-bats do you?"

Mr. Rose calmly shared his philosophy with the throngs of reporters who were anxiously awaiting his justification for this seemingly boastful claim. "Every time I step up to the plate, I expect to get a hit! If I don't expect to get a hit, I have no right to step in the batter's box in the first place!" If I go up *hoping* to get a hit," he continued "then I probably don't have a prayer to get a hit. It is a positive expectation that has gotten me all the hits in the first place."

> "People usually see what they are looking for and hear what they are listening for."
> **Harper Lee**

What we look at, and how we look at life is critical to developing correct beliefs and their subsequent actions. Your observation about what you see triggers your belief. That which you continually look at and talk about, you will most often receive. If you focus your observations on what you can't do and how you are not very good at doing it, you should not be surprised when this self-fulfilling prophesy comes true.

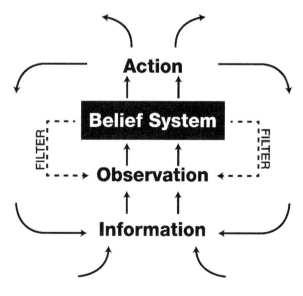

The *Hungry* Belief System diagram reinforces my admonition to guard what we look at because our belief and subsequently our actions will consequently be affected. A great deal is involved in looking at or collecting observations about something. Our brains contain a reticular activating system or RAS which, among other things such as regulating our sleep cycles, causes us to react very selectively to certain classes of stimuli. When we decide to sell our home we see *For Sale* signs everywhere because our RAS creates this subconscious priority of focus.

> "People are always blaming their circumstances for what they are. I do not **believe** in circumstances. The people who get on in this world are the people who get up and look for the circumstances that they want, and if they can't find them, make them."
>
> **George Bernard Shaw**

You can deliberately program your reticular activating system by choosing the exact messages you send from your conscious mind. For example, you can set goals with voice affirmations or visual cues. Napoleon Hill said that we can achieve any realistic goal if we keep on thinking of that goal, and stop ourselves from thinking any negative thoughts about it. Of course, if we keep thinking that we can't achieve a goal, then our subconscious will correspondingly help us to keep from achieving it.

Your reticular activating system cannot distinguish between *real events* and *synthetic* reality. In other words it tends to believe whatever message you give it. Imagine that you're going to be giving a speech. You can practice giving that speech by visualizing it in your mind. This pretend

> "Do you believe you're a starter or a benchwarmer? Do you believe you're an all-star or an also-ran? If the answers to these questions are the latter, your play on the field will reflect it. But when you've learned to shut off outside influences and believe in yourself, there's no telling how good a player you can be. That's because you have the mental edge."
>
> **Rod Carew**

practice should improve your ability to give the speech. When Stephen Covey says: "You can't talk yourself out of a problem you behave yourself into" he is articulating that behaviour comes from beliefs that take time to develop.

Steve Siebold says in *Secrets of the World Class*: "... average people are saddled with a set of beliefs that are more about survival than success. Average people have been programmed to avoid pain at all costs, which promotes a "playing not to lose" mentality... A world-class belief system is a primary factor in the making of a champion, and every great performer knows it." Believing is fundamental to establishing your *hungry* foundation and may be the one ingredient that, when applied to your Inner Game, gives you the largest incremental benefit.

Believe We Can

For more than one hundred years, runners tried to break the four-minute mile. Many said it couldn't be done. It was considered the "Holy Grail" of track and field. In fact, doctors wrote articles in medical journals explaining why it was physically impossible for the human body to run a mile in less than four minutes.

> "You may believe that you are responsible for what you do, but not for what you think. The truth is that you are responsible for what you think, because it is only at this level that you can exercise choice. What you do comes from what you think."
>
> **From *A Course in Miracles***

However, in May 1954, a British medical student named Roger Bannister ran the mile in 3:59.4. His amazing accomplishment made headlines around the world. Yet what happened afterwards is even more amazing. The four-minute mile was broken again the next month ... and then again ... and again. It has since been broken more than 700 times, sometimes by several people in the same race.

What happened? The runners weren't training any differently, but for the first time they believed they could do it. The barriers to the mind had come down. Other runners now *believed* it was possible.

The Power of Belief

In his article, "The Power of Belief," Mac Anderson admonishes us to: "Never underestimate the power of belief when it comes to fulfilling your dreams. I can say with no hesitation that every person I've ever met who has achieved any degree of success has had one thing in common: they believed with all their heart that they could do it. Early in my career, I was the vice president of sales for a food company. One time I was in Detroit hiring a salesperson. We had lined up eight appointments for the day, and the morning had been a bust. I looked up and my one o'clock appointment was standing at the door. He was a tall, good looking guy, and I remember thinking, "This could be the one." We talked for about 15 minutes, and I asked a question I always ask, "What will you be doing five years from now?" I'll never forget his answer. He said, "Mr. Anderson, the way these appointments are going I might still be interviewing!" Well, that wasn't exactly what I wanted to hear. We talked for a few more minutes and I excused him.

Then I looked up and my two o'clock was there. He walked over and gave me a confident handshake, and a few minutes

> "Whether you believe that you can or you can't... you're right."
> **Henry Ford**

later I asked the same question, "What are you going to be doing five years from now?" He looked me right in the eyes and said, "Mr. Anderson, I'm going to be working for you. This job fills my skills and my needs to a tee. I don't think, I know I can sell your product in this market. And furthermore, if you don't like my performance after 30 days, you don't owe me a cent." Well, you could have knocked me over with a feather! He had just made me an offer I couldn't refuse. But the offer had nothing to do with money I might earn; it had everything to do with his unwavering passion and belief he could do it. Within a year, Sam was the number one sales person in the company."

Over my years I have discovered that there is a very fine line between solid self-belief and a cocky, selfish attitude. People who are supremely confident, and do it the right way, work very hard not to boast about themselves to others. Insecurity often exposes itself in how much we talk about "our achievements" and how well we have been doing. Self-belief keeps from cloaking itself as cockiness by focussing our conversation on adding value to others.

Self-Belief

Self-belief is what we call self-confidence in professional sport. In *Simply the Best: Players on Performance*, co-written with Portland Winterhawk's GM and Head Coach Mike Johnston, I asked 7 elite hockey players how self-belief relates to their personal high performance. Phoenix Coyote captain and leading scorer Shane Doan answered, "I wish I knew! If you ask any player, they'll agree with this: If I score a goal in the first period, I am going to be twice the player; you are going to have your hands full trying to stop me for the rest of the game. It's so important in the NHL to have a tandem of two guys going on a team, because there are going to be nights when a guy doesn't have it, and all of a sudden he gets an empty net and he gets his confidence. If a centre makes a great play and gives you an empty net and you score, but you really didn't do anything other than put the puck in the net, you still get a boost of confidence.

> "If you have no confidence, you are twice defeated in the race of life. With confidence, you have won even before you have started."
>
> **Marcus Tullius Cisero**

It comes back to what we were talking about earlier; it's the confidence to believe that you are that good player and not the player that's struggling. I guess that's mental toughness too. I think those go hand in hand. Confidence is about really believing that I'm the guy who can score, the guy who can go out and dominate a game, the guy who can go out and have a game where everything works. That's who I am. The player who just turned the puck over or made that mistake is not me.

> "Don't lower your expectations to meet your performance. Raise your level of performance to meet your expectations. Expect the best of yourself, and then do what is necessary to make it a reality."
>
> **Ralph Marsto**

That's not who I really am. It's hard to continually have that level of confidence, but if you could ever master it, you would be a more consistent and durable player. You often hear players say when they aren't scoring, 'I can't score.' Very rarely do you hear guys say, 'I can score; I can score.' I think that the guys who are good truly believe that they can score. They just believe that. They have such confidence that they don't care if you stop them a hundred times, they still believe they are good enough to score. There are other guys who are more talented, but they aren't so sure they can score. They could score on you 10 times, but if they miss three or four in a row they literally believe that they can't score. I believe the difference is training your mind, and that comes back to mental toughness, where you say to yourself, 'I'm the guy who can score, not the guy who can't.'"

I'd like to pass on a gift from the world of sport that you can apply to the rest of your life! In his excellent sports psychology CD series called *The Maverick Mindset,* Dr. John Eliot explains that water skiing is basically comprised of 2 main components and a connection: the boat and the skier are connected by a rope. The skier may move slightly off course, but essentially, if the boat goes left, the skier eventually goes left, and if the boat turns to the right, the skier has no choice but to go right. This provides a tremendous analogy to the area of self-belief that the world of sport calls *confidence*. Most of us have a tendency to put our performance on the boat and our self-belief on the ski. If we choose to put outcomes or performance on the boat, we are allowing our emotions and our self-worth to be influenced and controlled by external indicators of how we are doing in life. What if we play our best game ever and our opponent beats us? Does this mean that our self-belief is going to be determined by our so called performance outcome?

Under this "performance driving the boat" scenario, when our performance is really good we really believe in ourselves. Our self-belief follows our performance: performance-up—self-belief-up; performance-down—self-belief-down. The problem obviously comes when we have poor performance and poor self-belief. Athletes will often go so far as to say that they have lost their confidence.

> "Part of being a champ is acting like a champ. You have to learn how to win and not run away when you lose. Everyone has bad stretches and real successes. Either way, you have to be careful not to lose your confidence or get too confident."
>
> **Nancy Kerrigan**

When we allow our self-belief to deflate we lose the ability to stay personally *hungry*! I wish that someone had shared this with me half-way through my NHL career. We need to change the process! Take self-belief off the ski and put it on the boat. Let your decision-making process drive. Then take performance and place it on the ski. Let it follow. Regardless of the environment we find ourselves in and regardless of our performance levels, we can choose to believe in ourselves. Self-belief, like courage, is influenced by environmental conditions but need not be *controlled* by them. Self-belief is a function of internal choice. Choice can be a wonderful ally if we don't abdicate our responsibility to enact its power.

One of the best examples of this boat/ski concept can be found by viewing our young Canadian and American soldiers in the

Middle East on the daily television news. If I was in this war zone, I would be so busy hiding from snipers and car bombs that I'm sure I would have great difficulty believing in myself. Yet I observe such a confident demeanor in these soldiers, as they focus on their jobs independent of the environment in which they find themselves. They have learned and are living the concept that they must choose to believe in themselves regardless of the environment.

People who accomplish their mission in life understand the necessity of prioritizing their Inner Game in order to execute their Outer Game. An incredible example of someone choosing to let self-belief drive the boat is encompassed in a story about US Senator John McCain. While in a Vietnam prison camp, John McCain decided that for a number of hours each day he would not be a prisoner. Instead, he created a new reality; he chose to be a professional golfer. McCain played 36 to 72 holes of golf every day. He played different courses and some nights stayed up late to finish his round. John McCain played golf every day for 7 years *in his mind*. When he returned to America people asked him what he wanted to do first. He was 50 lbs. underweight and they thought maybe he would choose a 5 course meal or to sleep on an amazing bed. Instead he said, "I want to play golf." Not only did John McCain survive as a prisoner of war, but in his first round of real golf outside of his imprisonment, he shot one over par.

It has been proven in basketball that practicing excellence in your mind is as important as practicing for real. Players who believe in their skills and themselves are more likely to initiate successful action. But

> "Once I get the ball, you're at my mercy. There is nothing you can say or do about it. I own the ball....When I'm on my game, I don't think there's anybody that can stop me."
>
> **Michael Jordan**

just as often, amazingly talented athletes underachieve because of their underdeveloped self-belief. Professional athletes increase their belief in themselves by practising being excellent at their craft… and so can you!

> "The only measure of what you believe is what you do. If you want to know what people believe, don't read what they write, don't ask what they believe, just observe what they do."
>
> **Dr. Ashley Montagu**

Believing is critical to confidence, and confidence essential to individual and team success. While interviewing the 12 NHL coaches for *SIMPLY THE BEST: Insights and Strategies from Great Hockey Coaches* to learn how professional coaches create high performance culture, we asked long time NHL coach George Kingston how he keeps players at their peak performance level. Kingston responded that "absolutely the most important thing that you need to have as a player is confidence. It is the expectation in yourself that you are able to perform, that you are able to do all the things that you have special gifts or special capacity for. Hockey is so competitive and it is so tough to be successful that it is hard for a player to maintain rock-solid self-belief, rock-solid confidence, and to avoid self-doubt."

When you are not winning or enjoying personal success, it may be an issue of poor self-belief. Nothing is more important than ensuring player and team belief. The most difficult championship to win in professional sport is the first one, because even professional players must believe that they can do it before actually accomplishing the success. This is, in fact, most of life! It has often been said that life is the opposite of school, because most of the time life gives you the test first and the lesson later.

During a family holiday our youngest son, Joe, pointed to a sign posted beside the pool where we were swimming. The sign read: "NO JUMPING, NO RUNNING, NO DIVING, NO SPLASHING." Joe turned to me and said, "Dad next time we come here it will probably say, NO SWIMMING!" The average child has been told "NO" or "YOU CAN'T DO THAT" 148,000 times by the time they are 18 years old. We are taught from a young age to focus on what we can't do, instead of on the things we expect to do. Setting expectations lifts our eyes and heart to the challenge of meeting them and believing that we can accomplish them.

When we believe the worst will happen, it often does. Warren Bennis calls this the Wallenda Factor, which demonstrates that believing can also make our fears come true. In 1978

> "When you believe and think "I Can" you activate your motivation, commitment, confidence, concentration and excitement- all of which relate directly to achievement."
> **Dr. Jerry Lynch**

Karl Wallenda fell to his death in downtown San Juan, Puerto Rico while doing what he did for a living, traversing wires. Mrs. Wallenda recalled, "All Karl thought about for 3 months prior to it… was falling. It was the first time he'd ever thought about it, and it seemed to me that he put all his energies into not falling rather than walking the tightrope."

Believe that you CAN!

The Man Who Thinks He Can

If you think you are beaten, you are
If you think you dare not, you don't
If you'd like to win, but think you can't
it's almost certain you won't
If you think you'll lose, you've lost
For out of the world we find
Success begins with a fellow's will -
It's all a state of mind.
If you think you're outclassed, you are
You've got to think high to rise
You've got to be sure of yourself before
You can ever win a prize.

Life's battles don't always go
To the stronger or faster man
But sooner or later the man who wins
Is the one who thinks HE CAN.

Anonymous

The "I CAN" is what we have to muster when our self-belief wanes. The average person generates between 2000 and 3500 thoughts per day, but 95% of them are the same thoughts they had the day before. Patterns of "I CAN'T" can easily become ingrained into our habitual life journey, and they become difficult to change.

Elite athletes, on the other hand, generate only 1500 thoughts per day. Contrary to popular opinion, this is not because they are not as smart! They have fewer thoughts because their thinking is more focused and they have managed to frame out (more on that later) many of the "I CANT'S" that the average person has permitted.

Since retiring from the NHL, one of the great projects I have enjoyed is partnering with Mike Johnston and his wife Myrna to write 2 books on high performance culture. Mike asked me to help him accomplish his dream to pull together some of the collective team and performance wisdom from NHL coaches and players. Mike has been an Associate coach with the Vancouver Canucks and LA Kings and is now Head Coach and GM of the Portland Winterhawks. Because of Mike's schedule at the time it became incumbent on me to interview most of these NHL coaches.

We asked Scotty Bowman, the NHL's most successful coach, "What was the thread that ran through all of your success?" Scotty has won 10 Stanley Cups, 9 as a head coach, coaching 4 different teams to 13 Stanley Cup finals. He hesitated for just a minute and then said confidently, "Ryan the thread that ran through all of my success was undoubtedly ownership's commitment to win." This may sound simplistic, but if the top leaders do not believe that winning is possible and make it a priority, then few other people in the organization get committed to make it happen.

Fan/Player

The *hungry spirit* thrives when we reduce complexity in order to simplify our game. The ingredient of Believing can be broken down into two main categories or patterns which describe the way we believe. The first I call Fan and the second, Player.

The fan is in the building but doesn't believe that he or she can ever fully participate. "This is for other people to do." The fan buys lottery tickets because he hopes for a win but doesn't feel empowered to pursue his personal win. The fan believes that she can't play because she might fail. Her life is relegated to cheering on those few brave souls who she believes were actually the only ones born to play. The fan holds on to limiting beliefs about himself and others, and like the sports fan in real life, pays a huge price of admission.

The player believes that it is up to him or her to get it done. The player believes that she controls the play and the pace and is empowered to not only make decisions, but believes that if she fails once in a while, it is part of the game. The player believes that he is a critical part of the team and feels accountable to others for his performance.

The Fan/Player analogy can easily be translated to Audience/Actor. Actors and audiences have different intentions. An actor is someone who participates in the action as opposed to the audience, who does not. The limiting belief of the fan or the audience says: "I could never do that."

I recognize that not everyone wants to act or play, but that's not the point. The point is these two general types categorize people's belief systems. The player believes that he or she CAN and the fan believes that he or she CAN'T. A fan's limiting beliefs often keep him on the sidelines.

From Fan to Player

Use your own ideas to fill out the following FAN/PLAYER worksheet. Identify what the fan believes and does in your culture (in the building… hoping for the win). Then identify the actions and beliefs of the player (in the action… believing and making things happen). Next spend some brain power on discovering how changes in the fuel of Believing can help you and your people avoid being merely fans and become firmly planted in the "I CAN" mindset of the player. Record (inside the arrow) how to keep your belief systems and your people's belief systems firmly planted in the Player's Zone.

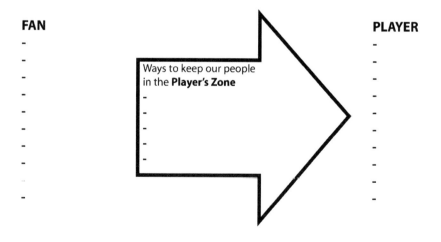

FAN
-
-
-
-
-
-
-
-
-
-

Ways to keep our people in the **Player's Zone**
-
-
-
-

PLAYER
-
-
-
-
-
-
-
-
-

Enhance your odds for tomorrow's success……by BELIEVING in your PLAYERS today!

Belief and Unbelief

"He stood on the side of the road and cried: 'Buy a hot dog Mister?' And people bought. He increased his meat and bun orders. He bought a bigger stove to take care of his trade.

He finally got his son home from college to help him out. But then something happened. His son said, 'Father, haven't you been listening to the radio and watching TV? There's a big depression. The foreign situation is terrible. The domestic situation is worse.'

Whereupon the father thought, 'Well, my son's been to college, he listens to the radio and watches TV and he ought to know.' So the father cut down on his meat and bun orders, took down his signs and cancelled his newspaper ads, and no longer bothered to stand on the highway to sell his hot dogs. And his hot dog sales fell almost overnight. 'You're right son,' the father said to the boy. 'We certainly are in the middle of a great depression.'"

-Author unknown

Brian Sutter, a player I played pro against and a long time NHL coach, told me that he likes his teams to start with 82 wins. He tells them at the start of the season to believe that they have 164 points in the bank account and he dares opponents to take any of them! Believing helps you maximize what you have, instead of dwelling on what you don't have.

Who Do You Believe In?

Winning cultures and teams are full of people who have learned how, and chosen to be, good teammates. Throughout my coaching career I have asked my players to do 3 things:

1. Focus your energies on what the team desires to accomplish.
2. Bring your very best to every practice and game.
3. Be a great teammate.

> "You were born to win, but to be a winner, you must plan to win, prepare to win, and expect to win."
> **Zig Ziglar**

Part of being a great teammate requires believing in your people. In *The Art of Possibilities* Rosamund and Benjamin Zander advocate a great practice for believing in the people you rub shoulders with daily. The authors call their idea "giving people an 'A.'" You can give an "A" to anyone in any walk of life - to a waitress, to your employer, to your mother-in-law, to drivers in traffic. When you give an "A" you find yourself speaking to people not from a place of measuring how they stack up against your standards, but from a place of respect that gives them room to realize themselves. This "A" is not an expectation to live up to, but a possibility to live in to.

The Zanders go on to say, " Michelangelo is often quoted as having said that inside every block of stone or marble dwells a beautiful statue; one need only remove the excess material to reveal the work of art within. If we were to apply this visionary concept to education, it would be pointless to compare one child to another. Instead, all energy would be focused on chipping away the stone, getting rid of whatever is in the way of each child's developing skills, mastery and self-expression."

Building *hungry* teams requires that people focus more on possibilities than problems. Human nature tends to keep our focus on what our teammates do wrong instead of believing what they can be. The idea of giving the "A" is a brilliant way to believe the best in our people.

The Monk's Story

"A monastery had fallen on hard times. It was once part of a great order which, as a result of religious persecution in the seventeenth and eighteenth centuries, lost all its branches. It was decimated to the extent that only 5 monks remained in the mother house: the Abbot and four others, each of whom were over seventy. It was clearly a dying order.

Deep in the woods surrounding the monastery was a little hut that the Rabbi from a nearby town occasionally used for a hermitage. One day it occurred to the Abbot to visit the hermitage to see if the Rabbi could offer any advice that might save the monastery. The Rabbi welcomed the Abbot and commiserated. 'I know how it is,' he said. 'The spirit has gone out of people. Almost no one comes to the synagogue anymore.' So the old Rabbi and the old Abbot wept together, read parts of the Torah and spoke quietly of deep things.

The time came when the Abbot had to leave. They embraced. 'It has been wonderful being with you,' said the Abbot, 'but I have failed in my purpose for coming. Have you no piece of advice that might save the monastery?' 'No, I am sorry' the Rabbi responded. 'I have no advice to give. The only thing that I can tell you is that the Messiah is one of you.'

When the other Monks heard the Rabbi's words they wondered what possible significance they might have. 'The Messiah is one of us, one of us here at the monastery? Do you suppose he meant the Abbot who has been our leader for so long? On the other hand he might have meant Brother Thomas, who is certainly a holy man. Or could he have meant Brother Elrod, who is so crotchety? But then Elrod is very wise. Surely he could not have meant Brother Phillip- he is too passive. But magically, he is always there when you need him. Of course he didn't mean me–yet supposing he did? Oh Lord, not me! I couldn't mean that much to you could I?'

As they contemplated in this manner, the old monks began to treat each other with extraordinary respect, on the off chance that one of them might be the Messiah. Because the forest in which it was situated was beautiful, people occasionally came to visit the Monastery to picnic or to wander along the old paths, most of which led to the dilapidated chapel. They sensed an aura of extraordinary respect that surrounded the five old monks, permeating the atmosphere. The people began to come more frequently, bringing friends, and their friends brought friends. Some of the younger men who came to visit began a conversation with the monks. After a while, one asked if he could join, then another, and another. Within a few years, the monastery once again became a thriving order, and –thanks to the Rabbi's gift–a vibrant, authentic community of light and love for the whole realm.'

Hungry people and *hungry* teams believe the best in each other and as they do, create a reciprocal *hungry spirit* throughout the organization. I am reminded of the biblical story about a father with a demon-possessed son. The disciples of Jesus could not remove the demon. When told about this Jesus said, "You unbelieving generation." When Jesus spoke with the father about his son, the father requested, "Jesus if you can, please help us." Jesus responded, "If I can? All things happen for the one who believes." The father has one of my favourite responses in scripture when he then says to Jesus, "I do believe… help my unbelief!" [Mark 10] Much of my time writing this chapter has been spent meditating on that thought.

Who Believes in You?

In February 2011 I participated in the Heritage Alumni game, part of the Heritage Classic weekend commemorating the rivalry between the 1986 and 1989 Montreal Canadiens and Calgary Flames. Cliff Fletcher, the GM of the Flames during those years, recounted how long-time NHL Coach Bob Johnson "**believed that NHL players could improve, and that belief drove everything that he did and implemented as a coach.**" Many of the leaders I deal with ask me the question: "Is leadership born or built?" My answer is BOTH! Some people may come out of the womb a little farther down the leadership skill and characteristic development road, but it really doesn't matter because great leaders continue to grow themselves in order to be their best.

For those who believe that leaders are only born, that belief will drive the way they approach spending their developmental dollars. I once coached with a person who didn't really believe that you could develop leadership in players, so guess how much energy we spent in this area? None! What we believe positions how we receive information and what action we take, including the way we deal with people.

One of my favourite actresses, Hilary Swank, was a teenager when her mom packed her up and together they headed to Hollywood. They had $75, a Mobil card, and no place to live when they got there. They lived in the car for a few weeks and then slept on the floor of a friend's house. Homeless, but never hopeless, Hilary began landing small parts.

Her big break came in 1999 with the starring role in *Boys Don't Cry*, which earned her an Oscar for best actress. "I'm just a girl from a trailer park who had a dream," she said at the Academy Awards. In 2005, with *Million Dollar Baby*, she became one of the few actresses ever to receive two Academy Awards. It wouldn't have happened without the dream and the drive to pursue it. "I was lucky enough to have a mom who said I could be anything I wanted in life!"

This is one reason that I always remind leaders that they have an amazing power in their possession which only activates when they give it away. Every day leaders have the opportunity to believe what people can be... instead of what people are. The power to believe in their people's future ability differentiates the greatest leaders from the rest.

What Difference Does Belief Make?

"Many years ago Gordon Thomas was a senior at a small college in Pennsylvania. He had been on the school's football team for 4 years, but had never played one down. His coach liked having him around because Gordon was the ultimate team player. Gordon was always the first player to practice and the last to leave. Gordon was always "up," and always encouraging everyone. As his coach said, 'Gordon is the glue that holds this team together.'

It was the Monday before the last game of the season, Gordon's last game as a senior, when the coach got the tragic news that Gordon's father had died from a sudden heart attack over the weekend. The coach called Gordon at home. Gordon rose above the tears to thank his coach for calling. His coach asked, 'Gordon, is there anything that I can do for you?'

After a long pause, Gordon said, 'Coach, I won't be able to be at the game on Saturday. I need to stay home with Mom and my sisters. Do you think the team could say a prayer for my dad before the game?' The coach promised that they would.

The day of the big game arrived. Two hours before kickoff, the coach was in his office when he heard a knock on the door. In walked Gordon, dressed in his uniform. 'Why aren't you home with your family?' the coach asked.

'Coach, I just had to be here today. Is the team still going to say a prayer for my dad?'

'Of course we will,' the coach said.

Gordon looked up and asked, 'Coach, could you please do me one favour?'

'Sure, son, anything.'

'Coach, I want to start today.'

'Start? You've never played a down in 4 years,' the coach blurted out. Then he realized the promise he had just made. Who knows why, but the coach had a soft spot in his heart for the kid who had just lost his dad. He figured that he'd put Gordon in for a couple of plays for the first set of downs and then take him out.

The coach kept his two promises. The team said the prayer and Gordon started.

On the second play of the game, the quarterback made a mistake and gave Gordon the ball. He ran 12 yards.

> "The state of your life is nothing more than a reflection of your state of mind."
> **Dr. Wayne W. Dyer**

The next play, Gordon got the ball again. He raced for 8 more yards.

Gordon played so well that the coach never took him out. Gordon had the type of game that football players dream about. He rushed for almost 200 yards and scored 3 touchdowns. He single-handedly won the game for his team.

Gordon was carried off the field on his teammates' shoulders.

What an amazing story! Gordon's last game was his first game— and it was his best game. When summoned to a post-game meeting with his coach, Gordon's first words were, "Coach, thanks for putting me in today!'

'Gordon, I never dreamed that you would play so well. What happened to you out there?' his coach replied.

After a long pause Gordon asked, 'Coach, did you ever meet my Dad?'

'No son I never had the pleasure.'

'Coach, the reason that you never met my Dad was because he never came to any of our games. My Dad was blind. And I believe that today was the first time he ever saw me play!'"

What Changed for Gordon that Day?

His talent and conditioning were the same (he wasn't good enough to be a starter). The team's system, team code, player personnel and coaching staff (all the things to help him be his best) were the same also. What changed for Gordon was inside him- **what he chose to believe changed**. His Inner Game changed. His desire to perform changed. His heart, his focus, his energy, his confidence all came together because what he believed changed.

Pastor Scott Dickie, a friend of mine, started a talk one Sunday morning by saying: "In two minutes the roof of this building is going to collapse." Everybody looked puzzled but nobody moved. Scott then made this observation to the congregation: "You didn't move or take action, because you didn't *BELIEVE* the information."

If your performance is not what you desire, check what you believe!

Using a pen or pencil, shade in how full your believing tank is today. How much do you believe?

What do I Believe Exercise:

Our mindsets are everything! Our belief system filters and directs our mindset, which creates our life focus and therefore our results. The following simple exercise for the end of this chapter is critical to staying *Hungry*. It will help you to answer the question: "What do I believe?"

What do I believe around relationships?

Are people out to get me?

_____

Do I trust people? Why or why not?

_____

_____

Should I allow people into my world? Why don't I?

_____

_____

What do I believe about my team?

What do I believe about my teammates? Are they good people or a bunch of thugs? Why?

_____

_____

Do I like my place of work? Why or why not?

_____

_____

Do I believe that my leaders are honourable or just looking out for themselves?

_____

_____

What do I believe about my family?

Are my children or brothers and sisters unconditionally loved, or do they have to work for my love?

_____

_____

Do I believe that my spouse or those closest to me are amazing people, or a nuisance zapping me of energy?

_____

_____

Finally, what do I believe about myself?

Am I worthy to achieve my very best? Do I have confidence in who I am and what I can be?

_____

_____

Do I believe that deep down inside (in my Inner Game) I am okay and at peace, and do I like myself?

_____

_____

Your answers to these questions can help you to shape your *hungry spirit* from your core. If you want to change your actions to get better results, first change what you choose to *believe*!

Leadership Tips

1. The difference between okay leaders and great leaders is that great leaders believe in what people can be, rather than what they are.

2. Leaders must develop strong personal beliefs around values and culture and team. Next leaders must believe that the direction and vision of their organization is correct and believe that it can happen. Leaders create the standard for belief. If they do not believe their organization can win, their unbelief is felt by the entire team.

INNER GAME ACTION SUMMARY

CORE FUEL

Purpose & Passion:	activates your HUNGRY CORE
Futuring:	activates your DESIRE to PURSUE
Believing:	activates your WILL to WIN

These 3 Fuel types are powerfully effective, completely synergistic in the way they work, and they feed off each other to keep the cycle going. **Purpose & Passion**, the compilation of your core strengths and what you are built to be and love to do, form the foundation of your Inner Game. **Futuring** sets your *hungry* energy flowing towards your desired destination. **Believing** unleashes your will. As you become *hungrier*, you increase your intention to fuel your Inner Game, which in turn initiates more *hungry* energy.

As you read through the Inner Game section, I asked you to record some of your thoughts and ideas in order to make each Core Fuel concept more personal to you. If you are having trouble writing in the book, then I highly recommend that you purchase the companion handbook so you can more easily work through these powerful exercises at **www.hungryfuellingyourbestgame.com/ handbook.** My desired goal is that you personalize the application of these principles and incrementally increase your performance because you did.

Each of these 3 Core Fuels is critical and warrants your attention. As you have already seen, you have the opportunity to fill in your personal fuel gauge for each fuel type at the end of each chapter. How full are your Purpose & Passion, Futuring, and Believing tanks? In other words, is each fuel type fully working to bring optimal health to your *hungry spirit*?

FREE GIFT!

For extra INNER GAME development, go online to our readers-only exclusive page:

www.hungryfuellingyourbestgame.com/innergame
password: innergame

OUTER GAME

PERFORMANCE
FUEL

Framing

Constructing

Rebounding

Chapter

Hungry Decision:
Framing

It's a Miracle

Over the years I have been amazed at the fun projects that have come my way. In the fall of 2002 I was approached by Rob Miller and Mark "Coach" Ellis, representatives of the Disney Corporation, to become involved in making the movie *Miracle*. During the course of the conversation I was asked to be the "hockey expert" for the film. The following spring was my first time behind the scenes of a major motion picture and one thing is true... they *eat* well.

I spent the good part of April, May and June 2003 working on the set, with many weeks' work on the ice prior to the actual shoot. *Miracle* recounts the true story of the amazing 1980 USA hockey victory over the Soviet Union, which eventually culminated in the Gold Medal Win. The chronicle, which has just been selected as the Number 1 Sports Story of the last 50 years in the United States, portrays the young, college-aged US team upsetting the older and more mature, dominating Soviet team.

My responsibilities with *Miracle* began with selecting and training the on-ice cast for the movie, and then ensuring that our team could replicate every important play from the actual  Olympics. I animated the plays, taught the plays, and practiced the plays with an outstanding group of athletes. Once the filming began, I also had the great pleasure of working alongside Kurt Russell, who did real justice to the role of head coach Herb Brooks. Kurt's desire to emulate Brooks' words and actions was awesome. He often sought my advice for help with developing authenticity of dialogue on the ice and on the bench, and even for authenticity of action (I was his body double for all of the rear angle skating shots).

I met many other great people as well, but I want to focus in on the director, Gavin O'Connor. He made a compelling movie, and did it with hockey integrity. I had often seen Directors looking through their outstretched hands or some device on TV, and I always thought this was just a Hollywood stereotype, enacted to garner attention. I soon discovered, however, that Gavin O'Connor would literally walk into the arena or dressing room set or on to the ice and have his hands up in front of him with the thumbs together on the bottom. He was constantly Framing in and Framing out. He would find the view that worked for him through his hands and then roll the camera. Gavin's focus was not only to frame in what he wanted in the movie, but also to frame out the things that he did not want moviegoers to see.

Framing Out

I spent enough time with Gavin O'Connor helping make the hockey side of the picture work, to be able to ask him in greater detail about this process of Framing. Gavin's perspective really impacted me. He told me that Framing *in* was easy, but that: "The hardest thing that movie directors have to do is *frame out*." Gavin went on to explain, "I have so many angles and backgrounds and stories that I desire to tell in and around this event that I could end up with an eight and a half hour movie that no one would watch."

Framing as a high performance tool doesn't happen only in the movie industry. My nine seasons as a player with the Montreal Canadiens were an amazing time of learning about values and expectations. In Montreal's hockey-crazed culture, if the Canadiens failed to win a championship in any given season, that season was a failure. This environment taught me quickly to control the "controllables." I cringe when I hear professional teams complain about issues that are outside of their control, like their opponents or the refereeing. I'm not saying that we didn't dislike some of the officiating; it's just that most of the time we chose to focus on controlling the "controllables."

During the 1980's and 1990's the Canadiens were one of the few teams that I knew of who housed their players in hotel rooms the day before a home game during the playoffs. Many of the players complained for awhile about not being able to see more of their families and not being able to sleep in their own beds, but after winning an important playoff round or better yet, a Stanley Cup, no one complained. What I witnessed was the Canadiens' management controlling the peripheral parts of the game that might, in the long run, give their team an advantage. Think about what they controlled that other teams left to chance. The first was sleep. Many of the players on our team had young families. We all know that there are times when even the most angelic kiddos don't sleep, and when they don't sleep, no one sleeps. Putting players in hotel rooms the night before home games ensured an important peripheral ingredient to winning—sleep! The second was nutrition. Most of us would have eaten well the night before the game but just in case, management was guaranteeing it. Finally, those extra dinners and breakfasts together created an enhanced team focus on our playoff games. Controlling the "controllables" can help frame out distractions while magnifying the positives inside the frame.

Framing out, then, is essential to increasing performance and sustaining your *hungry spirit*. During our 21st Century sprint we all have more balls in the air than at any other time in history. Do you remember the promise that technology was going to *free-up* our lives? By making us more accessible it has actually increased the pace of whatever game we play.

The question you must ask about the fuel of Framing is: to really stay *hungry* what should *not* be in your frame today, this week, or this month? Would consistently eliminating these one or two things increase your focus and inspire your *hungry spirit*? Framing is not just about all the positives that we choose for our team and ourselves. It is also about the things that we choose to frame out.

Peter Bregman shared a study in *Harvard Business Review* in which the Virginia Tech Transportation Institute put cameras in cars to see what happens right before an accident takes place. They found that in 80% of crashes the driver was distracted during the 3 seconds prior to the incident. In other words, the driver lost focus, by dialing a cell phone, changing a radio station, taking a bite of a sandwich, or maybe checking a text, and failed to notice that something had changed in the world around them. Then they crashed.

The world is changing fast and if we do not stay focused on what lies ahead by resisting distractions, we increase our chance of crashing. When I read Bregman's two lists to bring us focus, I was immediately reminded of the concept of Framing.

> **"List #1- Your FOCUS list** (the road ahead)
> What are you trying to achieve? What makes you happy? What's important to you? Design your time around those things, because time is the one limited resource; no one yet has worked 25/8.
>
> **List #2- Your IGNORE list** (your distractions)
> To succeed in using your time wisely you must ask the following questions: What are you willing not to achieve? What doesn't make you happy? What's not important to you? What gets in the way?"

Bregman suggests that most people have the first list but few have the second. With the speed of our lives, our distractions have increased ten-fold, so the second list is becoming more important than ever. He recommends that we don't make the lists and then shove them in our top drawer; rather these two lists should be part of our daily road map. What's the plan for today? How will

I spend my time? How will it further my focus? How might I get distracted? Then follow through and have the courage to live the answers to these questions.

A CEO friend of mine runs a billion dollar company that has just recently been purchased by a multi-billon dollar conglomerate. My friend's entrepreneurial mantra for all those early years was about creating an atmosphere of "what's possible?" "What should we do?" In essence, he wanted them to focus on what should be inside their frames. He was telling me that since the multinational took over he finds himself asking his people, because of all the meetings and bureaucracy, "what shouldn't you be doing?" He is now asking them to focus on Framing out some of the time-wasters that this new bureaucracy brings. There comes a time, while developing high performance, when leaders need to utilize both aspects of Framing.

Since my work on *Miracle*, I notice that my Reticular Activating System is hard at work identifying the concept of Framing all around me, though it is often called by other names. *Good to Great* author Jim Collins wrote in *USA Today*: "Suppose you woke up tomorrow and received two phone calls. The first phone call tells you that you have inherited $20 million, no strings attached. The second tells you that you have an incurable and terminal disease, and you have no more than 10 years to live. What would you do differently, and, in particular, **what would you stop doing?**"

That assignment became a turning point in my life, and the "stop doing" list became an enduring cornerstone of my annual New Year resolutions – a mechanism for disciplined thought about how to allocate the most precious of all resources: time.

A lesson came back to me a number of years later while puzzling over the research data on 11 companies that turned themselves from mediocrity to excellence, from good to great. In cataloguing the key steps that ignited the transformations, my research team and I were struck by how many of the big decisions were not what to do, but what to stop doing.

In perhaps the most famous case, Darwin Smith of Kimberly-Clark – a man who had prevailed over throat cancer – said one day to his wife: 'I learned something from my cancer. If you have a cancer in your arm, you've got to have the guts to cut off your own arm. I've made a decision: We're going to sell the mills.'

At the time, Kimberly-Clark had the bulk of its revenues in the traditional paper business. But Smith began asking three important questions: Are we passionate about the paper business? Can we be the best in the world at it? Does the paper business best drive our economic engine?

The answers came up: no, no and no.

And so, Smith made the decision to stop doing the paper business – to sell off 100 years of corporate history – and throw all the resulting resources into the consumer business (building brands such as Kleenex), which came up yes, yes and yes to the same questions.

The start of the New Year is a perfect time to start a stop doing list and to make this the cornerstone of your New Year resolutions, be it for your company, your family or yourself. It also is a perfect time to clarify your three circles, mirroring at a personal level the three questions asked by Smith:

1. What are you deeply passionate about?
2. What are you are genetically encoded for – what activities do you feel just "made to do"?
3. What makes economic sense – what can you make a living at?

Those fortunate enough to find or create a practical intersection of the three circles have the basis for a great work life."

G. Fairhurst draws attention to the photographer who frames the photo to capture his viewpoint for others to understand and appreciate: "Consider Dorothea Lange who photographed images from the Great Depression. She wanted to show the mood or plight of Americans affected by those hard times. Lange did not take pictures of empty factories, abandoned farms or large throngs of unemployed people. Instead, she placed her viewfinder into the faces of the people of the Great Depression. Her message was clear because she framed the Depression in terms of the individuals who were suffering. Ansel Adam's message was the message of the grandeur of the Big Country-space for heart and imagination, as he once suggested. Adams did not dwell on the solitary flower or a ploughed field; there were no side trips into little things. On the contrary he placed enormous vistas in his viewfinder. Both Lange and Adams are great photographers not because of their subjects but because of their skill at [**framing**], at transmitting their point of view.

> "That which holds our attention determines our action."
> **William James**

Just like the photographer, when we select a frame for a subject we choose which aspect or portion of the subject on which we will focus. When we choose to highlight some aspect of our subject over others, we make it more noticeable, more meaningful and more memorable to others. For this reason frames determine whether people notice problems, how they understand and remember problems and act upon them."

Framing is about selecting where and what to focus our attention on, as well as the attention of others. It is an incredibly important leadership skill to master. A plumber once used his backhoe to look for a broken sewer line under a neighbour's lawn and was successful in his search. When asked by the lady of the house,

"How can you stand that stifling smell?" His reply was "Smells like bacon and eggs to a plumber, ma'am." The plumber's frame of the situation, focusing on the economic gain, helped him tolerate the smell. Over the past 20 years I have focused most of my non-professional time on coaching our 3 boys in minor sports. I always chuckled when the players' mothers came into the dressing room, curled up their noses, coughed and exclaimed, "Eeew, it smells awful in here!" I always responded with, "What smell?" I have been in so many dressing rooms throughout my lifetime, and loved being there so much, that I literally never smell anything bad. As we continuously hold focused areas of our lives in our frame, our mind and body adapts to make them happen.

Our Frame of Reference

I recall reading the story of a man who played his violin at a Metro station in Washington, D.C. on a cold January morning. He played six Bach pieces for about 45 minutes. During that time, since it was rush hour, thousands of people went through the station, most of them on their way to work.

After the first three minutes a middle-aged man, noticing that there was a musician playing, slowed his pace, stopped for a few seconds, and then hurried on to meet his schedule. A minute later, the violinist received his first dollar tip from a woman who threw the money in the hat without stopping. A few minutes later, a man leaned against the wall to listen, then looked at his watch and started to walk again, clearly late for work.

The one who paid the most attention was a 3 year old boy. His mother tried to hurry him along, but the child insisted on stopping to look at the violinist. Finally, the mother pushed hard and the child walked forward, but kept his head turned toward the violinist all the time. This action was repeated by several other children. All the parents, without exception, forced their children to move on.

During the 45 minutes the musician played, only 6 people stopped and stayed for a considerable amount of time. Approximately 20 people gave him money, but continued to walk at their normal pace. He collected $32. When he finished playing and silence took over, no one noticed it. No one applauded, nor was there any recognition.

No one knew that the violinist was Joshua Bell, one of the greatest violinists in the world. He played one of the most intricate pieces ever written on a violin worth 3.5 million dollars. Two days before playing in the subway, Joshua Bell had sold out a Boston theater where the seats averaged $100. His incognito Metro station performance was organized by the Washington Post as part of a social experiment about the perception, taste and priorities of people.

If we do not have a moment to stop and listen to one of the best musicians in the world, playing the best music ever written on one of the world's finest instruments, how many other important things are we Framing out? Our frame often holds certain conditioned references. Most people's frame-of-reference considers musicians in Metro stations to be "bums looking for handouts," a frame of reference that might be blocking out the best music they have ever heard.

Frame In–Just the Essentials

I was traded to the Canadiens a short time before Scotty Bowman, the "winningest" coach in NHL history, had moved on to coach the Buffalo Sabres. Despite missing being coached by him, I have bumped into Scotty over the years and I have cherished our conversations. After our phone interview for *SIMPLY THE*

BEST: Insights and Strategies from Great Hockey Coaches, Scotty shared a story with me about Tiger Woods. Scotty told me he had always wanted to score a PGA round. When a PGA tournament came close to the Detroit area Scotty was invited to be an official scorer and was given the Tiger Woods foursome.

As Scotty was telling me this story I could feel the excitement in his voice. Scotty had been inside the rope, 25 feet away from Tiger and his peers for the whole day. At the end of the round Scotty headed into the scorers' tent only to see Tiger Woods adding up his scores. Tiger and Scotty knew each other from previous events and as Scotty walked into the tent entrance, Tiger said, "Scotty what are you doing here?"

By this point in our phone conversation Scotty Bowman was giggling as he said, "Ryan, I was 25 feet away from him for the full day and he never saw me." That is how disciplined Tiger's frame was. We get what we look at. What was in Tiger's frame to create exceptional high performance? Three words: JUST THE ESSENTIALS.

Focused Action Wins!

Movie Directors don't say:

Quiet on the set... ready, THINK! The storyboarding, preparation and thinking are already done.

Quiet on the set... ready, HESITATE! Not with the daily costs to shoot so high.

Directors behind the scenes of multimillion dollar movies simply command:

Quiet on the set...ready, ACTION!

At the end of the day, making movies demands ACTION! What actions are you taking today that add to the plot of the movie you desire to make, rather than the movie you end up with? Carl von Clausewitz said, "There is no higher and simpler law of strategy than keeping one's forces concentrated. In short, the first principle is: act with the utmost concentration." Daily concentration on the action in our frame gives us our desired outcomes.

The Ultimate Framing Challenge!

It seems to be human nature to immediately focus on what might happen instead of keeping our focus on "practicing the details that give us the win." I have had the distinct honour of playing in over 100 NHL playoff games. At some point almost every team will find itself at the brink of elimination in a best of 7 playoff series. This presented the ultimate Framing challenge for me. My mind naturally tried to migrate to: "Well, if we lose this game and don't move on, at least we have had a pretty good run." Over 11 playoff seasons, especially the two seasons when our team went all the way to the Stanley Cup finals, we learned through experience that to win we must force our focus onto what gives us the win, rather than focusing on what might happen should we lose.

Using a pen or pencil, shade in how full your Framing tank is today. How well are you prioritizing your action?

Frame in what you wish to have, what you want to experience, and who you want to become, rather than dwelling on what you don't have, don't want, or are afraid of becoming. What you choose to frame in is incredibly important, but what you frame out may be essential to being your very best. **You are making your life's movie one frame at a time**. Is it the movie you want?

Write down the 5 actions that should not or need not be in your frame this week:

1. _____

   _____

2. _____

   _____

3. _____

   _____

4. _____

   _____

5. _____

   _____

What are the 5 actions that must be in your frame this week?

1. _____

   _____

2. _____

   _____

3. _____

   _____

4. _____

   _____

5. _____

   _____

Leadership Tips

1. Great leaders intuitively spend time and energy Framing in the actions which move their people forward, and Framing out the obstacles which hold their people back. Basketball coach Phil Jackson

answered the question: "Why are you so good?" with: "I PAY ATTENTION!" Framing demonstrates the way leaders pay attention. A leader's responsibility is primarily to prioritize action and coach high performance. Effective leaders sharpen their team's focus through the vital art of Framing.

2. Framing must become personal first for leaders. Many leaders that I know want to manage events rather than lead people. Framing has to be a personal exercise before it can be a corporate exercise. Leaders must establish what should be in and out of their own frame before they can prioritize their people's energy. If you would like to fine-tune this area, you can work through the personal Framing process in context with the other exercises in the companion Hungry Handbook to gain a solid foundation as a leader (www.hungryfuellingyourbestgame.com/hungryhandbook).

FRAMING
activates your PRIORITY of ACTION

Chapter

Hungry Environment:
Constructing

HUNGRY

Working on a Dream

Twelve years ago my wife, Jenn, and I decided to build a new home. We purchased 2 ½ acres of view property and spent the next 10 months making decisions over everything from blueprints to water faucets. Our shared dream had always been to live in log. The Pacific Northwest has huge trees and after many trips to Whistler BC, host to the 2010 Winter Olympics, we decided to build with a combination of massive Western Red Cedar and Douglas-fir. Twelve years later we are still amazed every morning and feel privileged to live in such a place.

People who play and stay *hungry* spend time Constructing the foundation and framework of their lives. One of the main reasons that Jenn and I decided to build our dream at that point in our lives (before we could pay it completely off) was because of the ages of our children. Our 5 kids were young. We wanted to construct an atmosphere that would be refreshing and exciting and supply amazing memories. In the words of an unknown writer: "You build your house and then it builds you!"

Environment is everything. During my time with the Capitals, from 1978 through 1982, hockey was not viewed as a top-tier sport in Washington, DC. The articles about our team's success (and lack of it) were placed at the back end of the sports section, next to the obituaries. What kind of atmosphere do you think that generated? Getting traded to Montreal in 1982 gave me a chance to experience the polar opposite. The Canadiens had just come off 4 Stanley Cup wins in the 70's and their sports coverage was massive. The team atmosphere matched it: upbeat, dynamic, and full of extremely high expectations. The *hungry spirit* has a much better chance of igniting in a superior atmosphere.

Environments that are dynamic seldom happen spontaneously, they have to be shaped and constructed. As a leader of yourself first, and then others, you are responsible for the atmospheric conditions of your culture. What kind of environment are you building today to help you and your team stay *hungry* tomorrow?

Hungry Context

During the winter of 2003 I was off on another early start to my day, heading to encourage and inspire leadership development with a client in Calgary, Alberta. The coffee pot in our bedroom went off at 4:45 AM; I was up at 5 and out the door by 5:45. Driving towards the airport to board a 7:30 flight, I had a coffee in one hand and the steering wheel in the other. BANG! I had just pulled into the passing lane as cars were merging onto the freeway in front of me, and a young deer sprinted out onto the highway into my path, and hit the right front bumper of my vintage BMW. Coffee flew everywhere and with my two hands struggling to hold the wheel, my car veered to the left, on to the middle median, and started heading toward the opposite lanes of oncoming traffic. I finally regained control of the car and pulled to a stop. In a split second my life had flashed before me, and the old Beamer that I loved was totalled.

Two thoughts hit me as I sat there waiting for the police and tow truck to come. The first was how rapidly outside events can impact and change our inside perspective and emotions. The second was how so much of our Outer Game is outside of our direct control. Remember that we can only control the "controllables." In my quest for the specifics of how to construct a superior performance environment, I have continually encountered the concept of *context*, which has been defined as:

1. the parts of a written or spoken statement that precede or follow a specific word or passage, usually influencing its meaning or effect: You have misinterpreted my remark because you took it out of context.

2. the set of circumstances or facts that surround a particular event, situation, etc.

According to Robert Cialdini, "It's what you do before what you do that counts." In other words, the context we create has a huge influence on the outcomes we get. The world of professional sport uses the word *atmosphere*. Coaches and executives who consistently win are constantly looking to understand and influence the temperature of their team's atmosphere.

Creating the context for *hungry* people and teams fascinates me. I have spent most of my life participating in and working towards enhancing the atmosphere which facilitates high performance and sustains a winning team. A former professor turned friend of mine, Matt Logan, used his PHD to help the RCMP crack criminal cases. In interrogating suspects, Matt learned that if the suspect emerges from the session feeling that he or she has gotten the upper hand on the investigator, this suspect must never be interrogated in the same room again. Matt ensures that his investigators always change the context for the suspect in any further interrogation sessions. He has observed that context has an impact on how people feel and respond. Similarly, during my playing days with the Montreal Canadiens, I watched companies hold their sales meetings within the confines of the Montreal Forum. These companies wanted their people to vicariously experience the Canadiens' *winning context*.

For 15 NHL seasons a myriad of smelly, intense, ego-driven dressing rooms continuously schooled me about the context of the *hungry spirit*. I experienced two very different environments during that time. The first was the environment that I couldn't wait to be part of. The second was the environment that I couldn't wait to leave. I have since learned that the talent and coaching and structure of organizations in today's marketplace can be similar to those dressing rooms. Great leaders pay attention to and intentionally construct an environment that their people can't wait to be part of.

Olympic decathlon gold medalist Bruce Jenner was said to have arranged his entire apartment so it would remind him every day of his goal. He put equipment from each of the ten sports in the decathlon in places where he couldn't help but encounter them during his non-training hours. Since the high hurdle was his weakest skill, he placed a hurdle right in the middle of the living room, where he had to step over it as many as thirty times a day. His doorstop was an iron shot. His barbells were on the patio. Vaulting poles and javelins rose from behind the couch. And his closets held the uniforms of his sport: sweat suits and running shoes. The unusual decor, Bruce said, helped him improve his form as he prepared for (and won) Olympic gold medals.

You can surround yourself with your dream and build your commitment in hundreds of ways. The method you choose is not important. Bruce Jenner's methods to establish his winning atmosphere were exceptionally imaginative and even extreme--but so were the results. *Futuring* taught you to keep your goals constantly in your peripheral vision. Ensure that you construct an environment that will help sustain the momentum required to accomplish your goals.

During the years that I coached in the NHL the Vancouver Canucks' ownership worked hard to change the atmosphere in and around the players' dressing room. The large open dressing room was turned into a smaller oval shape to be more inclusive, with fewer corners where players could hide. They constructed a large kitchen and breakfast nook so players could feel more at home. Technology was improved, colours were changed, and calculated improvements were implemented to help create an atmosphere where players were so comfortable that they wanted to stick around.

Progressive leaders who create upbeat, exciting culture are being thermostats instead of thermometers. Anyone can take the temperature and notice that their culture is cold. *Hungry* leaders intentionally improve their team's context.

Before building our house Jenn and I dreamed about things that would create the environment that we knew would then shape our family's life. We hit a home run with one extra addition to our master bedroom. We decided to put in a gas fireplace with two chairs in front of it, and a coffee maker within arm's reach. Brilliant! For the past 12 years, every morning we can't wait to get up to a warm fire and a cup of coffee and the shared beginning of a new day.

Atmosphere is everything! Our family decided a long time ago that purchasing books or any learning material would always be outside of any budget that we were adhering to. In other words if you live in our home and you want to purchase a book, no questions asked, you get it. We desired deeply to develop a life-long environment of learning.

Independent of the money we have to spend, however, we can choose to construct an environment that will help us win our Outer Game. Charles Tremendous Jones wisely said: "You will be tomorrow the books you read and the people you hang out with, today." Thank you, Charlie. These are two simple steps that we can take today which cost little or no money. A large part of Constructing the right atmosphere comes from deciding who the right people are for you. Whether you hang with ducks who squawk or eagles who soar, you will become one. A friend of mine, speaker and author Joe Roberts, told me: "There are two types of people - The *more* people and the *enough* people. Some always want more performance, others say what I am and what I am doing is good enough." Which type do you think we should hang with in order to stay *hungry*?

It costs us nothing to surround ourselves with constructive people and to frame out those who are destructive. It similarly costs us nothing to borrow books, either from our constructive teammates or from the library. I love to ask leaders I admire about the books they are reading (or listening to), and seek those books out for myself. *Hungry* leaders are voracious readers. Whether it is books or people, the essence of *Hungry* construction is you've got to want to do it!

Looking back I can see the difference a *hungry* context made in my life. During the early part of my high school years I had amazing friends but for us, C- was good *enough*. I moved away from home when I was 15 years old and fell into a crowd that focused intently on 2 things: excellence in school and hockey. Guess what happened? I got *hungry* and my marks went through the roof. I know that I didn't get smarter; this was the same old me doing homework. What changed was my intensity towards the homework, a direct result of my new context.

When I asked Olympic Women's Hockey great Hayley Wickenheiser about how to construct a *hungry* environment, she responded: "Players can really influence it or hurt it. I believe it takes 20 players to create a winning environment, but only one to wreck it. One player with a bad attitude can really affect the team in a negative way and it probably takes five or six players to make up for that. To keep that positive energy it's always a challenge to keep the negative away from the dressing room as much as possible. We always talk on our team about energy takers and energy givers. Some days you're not going to be your best when you show up at the rink or are on the ice, but trying to always give something positive no matter what is key to a successful team."

John Maxwell says, "Leadership is influence!" Leaders either take intentional steps to influence the culture they desire or leaders, by-accident-on-purpose, wake up to a culture they don't like. Players either supply energy to the team or suck energy from it. *Hungry* teams and *hungry* cultures harbour players who desire to contribute, compete, and are committed and accountable to being their absolute best. They are in this state in large part because of the atmosphere created by both their leaders and their team.

Small positive steps can also enhance your personal and cultural environment as my friend, Ward Clapham, demonstrated. Ward hired me to do leadership development for some of his Royal Canadian Mounted Police Officers in Richmond, British Columbia, where, like many other parts of the world, the growth of antisocial behaviour and crime amongst youth was increasing. Senior management recognized that traditional law enforcement alone would not solve the crime and disorder complexities that they were facing. The old paradigm of reacting to crime was no longer working. The methods that once produced safe streets and safe homes were now failing, not because of inadequacies or incompetence, but because the problems themselves had changed. The Richmond RCMP started to proactively discover alternative solutions that could *prevent* youth crime wherever possible.

One of the things that Ward implemented to change the atmosphere to reduce criminal behaviour was what he coined, "Positive Tickets." Positive Ticketing is a community program in which kids who are caught doing good things or staying out of trouble are rewarded by police officers and caring adults with a voucher to enjoy a fun, free activity. Over 40,000 positive tickets are given out by police and community members each year. Ward and his colleagues found a way to foster good behaviour by rewarding people for doing what is right, instead of only punishing what is wrong. I encourage you to read more in Ward Clapham's two great books, *Positive Tickets* and *Lead Big*.

The Intersection of Leadership and Team

Our Outer Game either slows to a stop… or accelerates to top speed at the intersection of Leadership and Team.

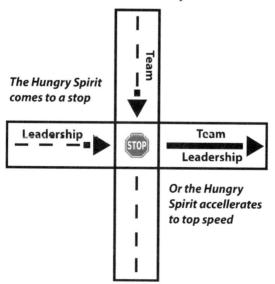

Highly impactful leaders partner with their teams to create optimal cultural momentum. South West Airlines and Synovous Corp. are famous for the *hungry* atmospheres they have created. Erin Moore of DuPont said: "I have seen all sorts of management fads come and go... by far, the most important factor in any organization's success is its ability to draw on its people's passions." Great cultures nurture and celebrate the *hungry spirit*. We can laugh at Will Roger's witty comment, "Even if you're on the right track, you'll get run over if you just sit there," but we know he's right! You are either taking small steps toward your desired culture or losing ground to people who have figured out how to stay *hungrier*.

Using a pen or pencil, shade in how full your Constructing tank is today. How inspiring is your environment?

Constructing Exercise

A great culture is revealed by the conversations of its people. Dan Britton and Jimmy Page, co-authors of *Wisdom Walks* each annually choose one word to flavour the atmosphere of their coming year's journey. Every year for the past 15 years, prior to New Year's Day, they have individually selected a word that will give meaning and focus to their lives for the year to come.

They don't just randomly pick it, but rather through reflection, prayer and listening to their hearts, the word comes to them. When we focus on words, they gain power. After some reflection, choose one word that will help you to flavour your personal atmosphere. Allow your word to be wrapped around you for one year.

You may want to borrow one of the following words or use them to trigger your own word:

PURPOSE, PASSION, FUTURING, BELIEVING,

FRAMING, CONSTRUCTING, REBOUNDING,

DEFLECTING, HONOURING, CONNECTING

Or how about this one… *HUNGRY*!

My WORD for this year is:

_____!

(My word for this year is breakthrough… breakthrough business barriers, breakthrough health, etc.)

Leadership Tips

1. "You build your house and then your house builds you." This is vital to leadership. Atmosphere is everything when it comes to building and leading high-performing *hungry* teams. Leaders who pay attention to what influences their people's thoughts and feeling are well on the way to Constructing a winning environment.

2. Let's take the Constructing exercise a little farther for you leaders. Describe in 10 words the kind of atmosphere or environment you desire to work in and have your people develop and grow in. Keep these key words in front of you every day for one month. At the end of one month, if these are the right words, find ways to get them into the middle of your culture. If they are the wrong words, change the words and start over.

For more Hungry Leadership/Constructing exercises go to www. hungryfuellingyourbestgame.com/hungryhandbook

CONSTRUCTING
activates your PERFORMANCE
ENVIRONMENT

Chapter

Hungry Again:

Rebounding

HUNGRY

Ouch!

I played junior hockey in Canada for the Langley Lords when I was 15 and 16 and then at the end of my 16 year old season was called up to play in the playoffs for the Kamloops Chiefs of the Western Hockey League. Early in my first game, I was driving around a big defenseman and

> "Obstacles are the challenges for winners and excuses for losers."
> **M.E. Kerr**

moving in on goal when the defenseman took my skates out from under me with his stick, causing me to slide hard into the goal post. If any of you are as old as I am, you will remember those posts. Why would anyone secure the post solidly under the ice? Anyway, my knee hit the post and promptly disintegrated.

Our team doctor and friend, Bob Smillie, explained that the operation was like sewing string-style mop heads together. Many people wondered if I would still be the same player for whom they had high hopes, after my long operation. Post surgery, the team doctors warned my folks that due to the significant damage to my knee, they could not guarantee that I would skate again. There are advantages to being a teenager when people tell you things that you do not want to hear; most teenagers don't believe what people in authority say anyway! And that, in this instance, was a good thing. After playing 1003 NHL games I am thankful to both doctors for their fine work on my knee and also thankful that at that point in my life I was *hungry* to prove the doctors wrong and play professional hockey.

> "Courage is rightly considered the foremost of the virtues, for upon it, all others depend."
> **Winston Churchill**

Upon reflection, I actually think that busting my knee at 16 years old helped me realize my NHL dream. The commitment that I had to muster to rehabilitate that knee increased my pain threshold and challenged my desire to be a player. It taught me how to rebound.

Be Thankful!

As I was writing this chapter, during the Christmas season, I believe I discovered the primary requirement for successful Rebounding. It can be observed first hand in millions of homes and children's hearts over the holidays. The key is to be like a kid on Christmas morning–thankful for the gifts you have received and optimistic and excited about the next new gifts that are coming your way. Truman Capote said, "Failure is the condiment that gives success its flavour." When we take our eyes off of our disappointment and get them focused on all the blessings that failure often brings, then we learn to stay resilient!

Herodotus wrote, "It is better by noble boldness to run the risk of being subject to half the evils we anticipate than to remain in cowardly listlessness for fear of what may happen." Stephen Covey challenges us to, "Live out of your imagination, not your history." They are both right, of course. Professional sport introduces athletes early to the necessity of "parking it." After a poor performance or a streak of losses players and coaches will remind each other that they must *park* the desire to remember and ruminate on the past, and turn to face the future opportunity.

> "History has demonstrated that the most notable winners usually encountered heartbreaking obstacles before they triumphed. They won because they refused to become discouraged by their defeats."
>
> **Bertie Forbes**

Handling Failure

The second requirement for successful Rebounding is recognizing that failure is not a person; it is an event. One of my favourite NHL coaches, Pat Quinn coached me for my final 2 NHL seasons with the Vancouver Canucks. A plaque on the wall of the coaches' room displayed this statement: "A failed project is not a failed person." The human tendency is to merge these two. When our project fails we feel we have failed as a person. Entrepreneurialism, because of its very nature to take risk, guarantees that failure is going to happen. The key is not to allow failure to stop our emotional forward momentum.

Just because our team loses, that does not mean that we are *losers*. This concept is critical to our self-belief and to keeping ourselves and our players *hungry*. If someone calls you a loser it's still up to you whether to believe what they say or not. From the beginning of this book we have vowed to work together to get ourselves to the next level. Next-level journeys very seldom happen without setbacks and obstacles.

My work training in the corporate world and coaching some of the world's top amateur and professional athletes provides me with ample opportunities to observe and understand my clients' sport and business pain across many sectors. As I help grow the leadership quotient on each of these teams, I guarantee leaders across the world only one thing: difficulty. I wish that I could guarantee each of them a lifetime of success, but I can't.

During difficult times leaders are always being watched. Over the course of our married life, when we have faced adversity, my wife, Jenn and I have tried to remain cognisant of the fact that our 5 children were always watching. How we reacted and resolved to get through each challenge would help shape the way our children would learn to stay resilient. Pericles said "What you leave behind is not what is engraved in stone monuments, but what is woven into the lives of others." Developing the skill of Rebounding always generates a strong ripple effect on the people closest to you.

Practice the Rebounds!

When I asked Sidney Crosby what effect adversity may have had on his development into an elite hockey player, he responded with: "My mental toughness came from being competitive and by trying to learn as much as possible from each experience. Everyone has their own way of dealing with adversity. For me, it was through learning how to approach things and being properly prepared." Being prepared comes from purposeful practice. This may be one of the large shortcomings of business when measured against sport. In professional sport athletes daily practice specific actions to increase their ability and efficiency, while business tends to focus on production. Fortunately, progressive companies are beginning to develop coaching and training to better practice and prepare their teams. Sidney is right! The more prepared we are, the better we can get ready for the rebound.

Basketball gives us the perfect mind visual. Watching basketball practices, you cannot miss how much of the time players practice this art of Rebounding. In sport, as in life, we don't always score on our first shot. Goaltending at the NHL level today is vastly improved because technique and equipment have accelerated a goalie's ability to stop shots. So, I am noticing a trend. Over the past 10 seasons, more NHL goals have been scored off the second shot than the first. In other words, we get our desired success off the *rebound*.

> "If you can find a path with no obstacles, it probably doesn't lead anywhere."
> **Bertie Forbes**

Be prepared for the gap between the practice and the success, though. Life, like sports, often has a lag time between your best performance and victory. Rest assured that with continued practice and optimal performance the gap will eventually be bridged and your rebound will find the back of the net.

Two Options

Life keeps coming and when it hits us hard we have two options:

1. **Have a Pity Party:** Like most people breathing, I'm pretty good at this one: "How could this happen to me? Why me? How could God allow this in my life?" Few of us have answers to these questions. The problem with the pity party is that it completely removes all responsibility and opportunity for us to create a solution. It gives control of our response away to luck. You recognize the second option well by now:

2. **Get *Hungry*:** The key to a successful recovery is not to roll with the punch, but to find that resilient energy and rebound hungrier than ever.

How to Rebound

My friend Tom Howse spoke of perseverance this way in a monthly message: "In the 1960's, Richard Attenborough decided to make a movie on the life of Mahatma Gandhi, and felt he could complete it in a few years.

Twenty years later, the movie was finally completed. Attenborough came close to bankruptcy, faced threats of riots in India, his star – Ben Kingsley – had never acted in a major film and received death threats for daring to portray Gandhi, and he was ridiculed by Hollywood studios who refused to invest in his project because, as one executive said, *'Who the **** wants to see a movie about a little brown guy dressed in a sheet carrying a beanpole.'*

> "The greater the difficulty... the more glory in surmounting it."
> **Epicurus**

Yet in 1982 *Gandhi* won 8 Oscars, including Best Picture (beating Spielberg's E.T.) and Best Director for Attenborough, who received a standing ovation from the very people who had ridiculed him. He attributes his success to "pig-headed determination," or simple perseverance.

Attenborough was inspired by Gandhi's perseverance, as well as the determination of his boyhood hero Winston Churchill, who, upon becoming Prime Minister in 1940 and facing an overwhelming enemy, said, "I have nothing to offer but blood, toil, tears and sweat . . . what is our aim. . . in one word: It is victory, victory at all costs, victory in spite of all terror, however long and hard the road may be."

We've all given up on worthwhile endeavours because they got too hard – a fitness program, a relationship, a business venture, a great idea, a New Year's resolution... You can make your own list. Sometimes cutting our losses becomes the right business decision, but more often than not our personal persevering comes before times of progress. For Rebounding to become second nature we must journey through difficult times learning the skill of perseverance.

Difficulty Gives Us the Opportunity to Rebound

"When an exploding bomb blew off the hands of paratrooper Harold Russell, he felt like his life was over. He had been looking forward to returning to his old job as apprentice to a butcher thinking that with a little luck he could end up being the manager of a butcher shop. Suddenly, no-hands, no-apprentice, no-job, no-future. Army doctors had fitted him with ingenious prosthetic appliances so that he could operate a typewriter, shoot a rifle and even thread a needle. He was far from

> "Success is to be measured not so much by the position that one has reached in life as by the obstacles which one has overcome."
> **Booker T. Washington**

being helpless, but he was hopeless, which was far worse. Not because of what happened to him but what happened in him. He thought that he had become a freak. When he was at the lowest ebb, psychologically, he was invited to make a training film to help other amputees. He was given the opportunity to help others similarly deprived. He buried his pride, his vanity, his concern about what other people might think of him. The rest is history. He signed a contract, to perform in the motion picture *The Best Years of Our Lives,* and became the only actor ever to receive two Motion Picture Academy Awards for an outstanding performance in a single film. Asked later whether he held any regrets about his condition, Harold Russell said, 'No. My deprivation has been my greatest blessing.' And he added, '**What counts is not what you have lost, but how you use what you have left**.'" The more life I have under my belt, I am less impressed by people's wealth and more impressed by people who get hit hard by life and rebound well.

Michael Jordan is recognized as one of the greatest NBA players of all time. It doesn't matter if you are a basketball fan or not, when you hear the name Michael Jordan your mind instantly takes you to the NBA record book, assuming that Jordan must be the best in free throw percentage or career points or points per game or most championships. As a matter of fact, Michael Jordan doesn't hold any of those records… he only holds one. Michael Jordan missed more shots than any player in NBA history! Failure is part of winning.

"You may not know the background of a certain laundry worker who earned 60 dollars a week at his job, but had the burning desire to be a writer. His wife worked nights, and he spent nights and weekends typing manuscripts to send to publishers and agents. Each one was rejected with a form letter that gave him no assurance that his manuscripts had even been read.

But finally, a warm, more personal rejection letter came in the mail to the laundry worker, stating that although his work was not good enough at this point to warrant publishing, he had promise as a writer and he should keep trying.

He forwarded two more manuscripts to the same friendly-yet-rejecting publisher over the next 18 months, and as before, he struck out with both of them too. Finances got so tight for the young couple that they had to disconnect their telephone to pay for medicine for their baby.

Feeling totally discouraged, he threw his latest manuscript into the garbage. His wife, totally committed to his life goals and believing in his talent, took the manuscript out of the trash and sent it back to Doubleday, the publisher who had sent the friendly rejections. The book, titled *Carrie*, sold over 5 million copies, and as a movie, became one of the top-grossing films in 1976. The laundry worker, of course, was Stephen King."

Henry Block, a mentor from afar, started a highly successful business. I approached Henry many years ago to potentially invest in our latest entrepreneurial venture. Henry looked at me, chuckled, and said, "I will invest in your third company." Henry knew from experience what I had yet to experience: most entrepreneurs lose 2 companies before figuring it out and becoming successful in their own right. To stay in the game long enough to experience success, entrepreneurs must learn the importance of Rebounding.

Rebound by Winning Your Losses

Professional golf is an intensely competitive sport with a miniscule margin between winning and losing. PGA tournaments are comprised of four rounds of 18 holes, played over a four-day period. There are four major tournaments each year – The U.S. Open, The British Open, The PGA Championship, and The Masters. The average margin of victory between 1980 and 2004 in *all* tournaments *combined* was less than three strokes – less than a one-stroke difference per day. However, from 2000 through 2004, the winner across all tournaments took home an average of 76% more in prize dollars than the second-place finisher.

Many Olympic event winners earn their victories by a measure of time or distance. In the majority of these events, the margin of victory between winning the gold medal and *no medal at all* is extremely small. During the 2002 Winter Olympic Games, the margin of victory between a gold medal and no medal at all was:

Men's Downhill Skiing	0.65 seconds
Women's Downhill Skiing	0.93 seconds
Men's Two-Man Bobsled	0.54 seconds
Women's Two-Woman Bobsled	0.58 seconds
Men's 500-Meter Speed Skating	0.26 seconds

Most of life has most of us in a close race. Very few people continually run away with the prizes. Losing by a small margin, though painful, means that you are close. Players rebound well when they look for the win in every loss. With small adjustments, renewed preparation, and the realization of how close most of us are, we harness the power of Rebounding.

I was drafted into the NHL by the Washington Capitals in 1978, fortunate enough to be chosen second in the world. In my second season with the Caps I was named captain and developed a close professional relationship with Abe Pollin, the owner of the team. Abe was a kind and industrious man who loved basketball and was just getting to know the game of hockey when we met. After my four seasons with the Caps came to an end, I truly appreciated receiving a phone call from Abe minutes after I was traded to the Montreal Canadiens.

A few years ago I had a gut feeling to call Abe, out of the blue. I had not been in contact with him for years and wanted to see how he was doing. Abe was surprised to hear from me and amazed at the timing of the call because he was just that evening about to receive the Washington DC Entrepreneur of the Year award. I said, "Abe, fabulous, I'm excited for you," and then a thought struck me. I continued, "Abe, if you are going to receive an award that means that you will have to give a speech. What will you talk about?"

Abe chuckled and answered, "I am going to share one quick story and then sit down. Let me share it with you." Abe told me the story of when he was 16 years old and had two best friends and one objective: he wanted to make the high school basketball team the following fall. All three boys had their eye on this goal and worked out, shot baskets, and ran. They were well prepared and ready to make the team.

Everything was on track until two days before tryouts. Abe paused and said, "Ryan, I chickened out. I chickened out. That fall I sat in the stands and watched my two best friends make and

> "Difficulties in life are intended to make us better not bitter."
> **Dan Reeves**

play for this team. All season long I watched other people do what I should have been doing. That season, at 16 years old, I swore to myself that I would never chicken out of life again. I would never watch someone else do what I should be doing. If I was supposed to do it, I would. Ryan, I believe this was a defining moment in my entrepreneurial spirit."

I asked the follow-up question: "Abe you're a billionaire; you're an entrepreneur; you have lost companies and sold companies. How much of the time did it work out for you?"

Abe laughed and laughed and said, "Ryan, 51%."

Our ability to rebound from the 49% of our failure gives us the opportunity to reach the 51% of our success. Amway's Richard DeVos said, "If I had to select one quality, one personal characteristic that I

> "Nothing in the world can take the place of persistence. Talent will not; nothing is more common than unsuccessful men with talent. Genius will not; unrewarded genius is almost a proverb. Education will not; the world is full of educated derelicts. Persistence and determination alone are omnipotent. The slogan "press on" has solved and always will solve the problems of the human race."
> **Calvin Coolidge**

regard as being most highly correlated with success, whatever the field, I would pick the trait of persistence," and author Albert Camus synopsised, "Life is the sum of all your choices." When life hits hard, choose not to let its disappointments send you down the river of self-pity, but rather, Rebounding up the road of resolve towards accomplishing your dreams.

Using a pen or pencil, shade in how full your Rebounding tank is today. How resilient are you?

Regrets into Rebounds Exercise

Looking back, what do you regret having given up on?

_____

_____

_____

_____

_____

_____

_____

How can you turn those regrets into rebounds? (for example, Abe vowed never to chicken out again)

_____

_____

_____

_____

_____

_____

_____

Leadership Tips

1. Sir Winston Churchill said, "Kites rise highest against the wind - not with it." Great leaders remain calm and get amazing things accomplished during difficult times. Leaders know that tough times will always come and prepare for them. Most leaders learn these Rebounding and perseverance skills by walking through difficult times in their lives. The learning opportunity through difficulty is to apply the lessons learned as we journey toward the next tough time.

2. People must see and sense a leader's resilience. Leaders who survive and thrive in the midst of difficulty are the leaders we want to follow. Remember that change is easier to make on the rebound than when things are going well.

OUTER GAME ACTION SUMMARY

PERFORMANCE FUEL

HUNGRY

Framing: activates your PRIORITY of ACTION

Constructing: activates your PERFORMANCE
                             ENVIRONMENT

Rebounding: activates your RECOMMITMENT

These 3 Fuel types power everything to do with your outer performance. **Framing** initiates your high performance by helping you to prioritize what you should spend energy on and what you should keep out of your frame. Distractions are the number one enemy of high performance! As you initiate **Constructing** a winning atmosphere, your performance is enhanced accordingly. Finally, by **Rebounding** you maintain your long-term performance success. Everybody runs into tough times. Our lives are defined by how well we rebound from them.

As you read through the Outer Game section, I asked you to record some of your thoughts and ideas in order to make each Performance Fuel concept more personal to you. If you are having trouble writing in the book, then I highly recommend that you purchase the companion handbook so you can more easily work through these powerful exercises at www.hungryfuellingyourbestgame. com/handbook. My desired goal is that you personalize the application of these principles and incrementally increase your performance because you did.

Each of these 3 Performance Fuels is critical and warrants your attention. At the end of each chapter you had the opportunity to fill in your personal fuel gauge for each fuel type. How full are your Framing, Constructing, and Rebounding tanks? In other words, is each fuel type fully working to bring optimal health to your *hungry spirit*?

FREE GIFT!

For extra OUTER GAME development, go online to our readers-only exclusive page:

www.hungryfuellingyourbestgame.com/outergame
password: outergame

TEAM GAME

Chapter

Hungry Motive:

Deflecting

Team Foundation

I have observed on and off the ice that two personal leadership actions create the strongest foundation for teamwork. The first is taking personal responsibility. The second is Deflecting personal glory. The former removes pressure from the team, while the latter adds power to the team. Together they have the potential to form an unbreakable bond.

Accepting Responsibility

As a 22 year-old captain of the Washington Capitals I made plenty of mistakes and errors in judgement, and the one I am about to share is right up there with the best of them. My teammate, Gordie

Lane, became a close friend. Once in awhile when our team was given a day off from practice, Gordie would pick me up in his pick-up truck and haul me off to Maryland's Eastern Shore for a day of hunting. I was never a hunter, but I loved to go along with him and enjoyed getting away. One day while we were driving I noticed that Gordie had 2 guns and 2 licences in the truck. When I inquired about this, Laner said, "Just in case." "Just in case of what?" I asked. He answered, "Just in case you want to shoot." I never thought any more of it.

> "If something goes wrong, I did it. If something goes right, we did it. If something goes really well, they did it."
>
> **Bear Bryant**

When we arrived at the hunting location, I hauled all of the stuff that we normally carried, along with the extra gun and licence. Throughout the day I may have shot once and certainly didn't hit anything but clouds. I didn't know what this meant, but I guess we "picked up a little late," and scrambling a bit, Gord grabbed the geese that he had shot. I'll never forget what happened next. Just as we were about to head to the truck, two men in pin-striped three piece suits stepped out of the bush, held up their badges and yelled, "Drop the guns--FBI."

Have you ever felt heat move progressively from the bottom of your feet to the top of your head? I did at that moment. In my hand I had a teammate, Dennis Hextall's licence. Dennis was 36 years old with red hair; I was 22 with brown hair. Now you can see my predicament. My friend, Laner knew exactly how much trouble I was in and started rolling on the ground, laughing so hard he couldn't speak. Needless to say the FBI were not impressed with me. Hundreds of dollars in fines later, I was finished with hunting for good.

Here's what I learned that day: none of it was Gordie Lane's fault. I had been given a choice to make and I made the wrong one. Personal responsibility can also be personal liability, depending on our choices. There is a tendency in North America to use the "blame-game," but leaders of *hungry* teams learn early to take personal responsibility.

Deflecting Credit

The culmination of the 2001 NHL playoffs saw Colorado Avalanche captain Joe Sakic receive the Stanley Cup from NHL Commissioner Gary Bettman. As Sakic took the Cup he did something very few captains in sports history have done. Instead of lifting it high over his head in celebration, Joe moved it sideways across his body and handed it to Ray Bourque, who with exhilaration, lifted the Stanley Cup high, brought it down, and gave it a huge kiss. Ray Bourque had been traded to Colorado after 17 seasons with the Boston Bruins. Ray Bourque had never won a Stanley Cup.

I was at home watching with my wife, Jenni Jingles and our kiddos, and was amazed at what we had just witnessed: *a sideways cup!* Joe Sakic told an amazing tale with his actions that night. What he did revealed the kind of unselfish leadership that empowers teams to win championships.

> "Build for your team a feeling of oneness, of dependence on one another, and of strength to be derived by unity."
> **Vince Lombardi**

Forgoing the glory of first lifting the Cup high above his head and passing that opportunity to Bourque instead, was something I felt compelled to investigate. The next season while I was in Denver to broadcast an NHL game, I asked Avs goalie and friend Patrick Roy about what I now called *The Sideways Cup*. Patrick knew exactly what I meant and said to me, "Wally, you wouldn't believe it. Weeks before we made it to the Stanley Cup final, every time Joe saw Ray he would say, 'Bourquie, when we win the Cup… make sure you stay close to me.'" The Avalanche players had found a cause to inspire their playoff run: "Let's win it for Ray."

Great leaders learn to focus on what is best for their team. The old sports adage claims that if you play for the name on the back of your sweater then nobody cares, but if you play for the name on the front of your sweater, everyone wants to know the name on the back of your sweater. This is so true! *Good to Great* author, Jim Collins says that humility is one of the overriding qualities of a top leader. Deflecting is the active progeny of humility. Feeding and sustaining the *hungry spirit*, at least in part, is less about focusing on me, and more about focusing on the Rays in my life! What is your cause or your team's cause? Who are you playing for?

> "My responsibility is to get my twenty-five guys playing for the name on the front of their uniform and not the one on the back."
>
> **Tommy Lasorda**

One training camp during my early years in Washington, my General Manager was incredibly high on another young player. As training camp continued I had the chance to play with this player a number of times. I could see that he had physical talent but I felt there was something lacking. Several weeks into our time together he said something to me prior to an exhibition game that confirmed what I was feeling: "Ryan, you get into the corner, pay the price to get and keep the puck, then you pass it to me, and I'll score the goal." The sad part of this whole scenario was that he really meant it! This player was bringing the wrong attitude to the NHL team table. If he wasn't willing to share in paying the price, then it just wasn't going to work... and it didn't. One month later he was released from the team. The attribute he was displaying was obviously the opposite of deflection. At its core deflection focuses on elevating others and not taking the credit. I am always amazed that attitudes like this player's often don't reach management sooner, and even coaches get fooled for a bit. But a selfish attitude is quickly revealed to those with whom we work closely.

Deflecting Conversation

How, then, do you deflect on a daily basis? So much effort goes into what you have to get done... and done now, that you may think you have little time left to implement this fuel. Still, I know many people who manage to live the quality of deflection, and their Team Games reap the benefit. One simple way to daily place your focus on other people can be found right, smack in the middle of your conversations. Implementing deflection can change everything for people who typically talk about themselves and what they have done, by taking the conversation flow off of "what I did," "how I'm feeling," and "my accomplishments" and Deflecting its flow toward the other person with "how are *you*?" "Where are *you* from?" What do *you* do?" The greatest leaders I have encountered ask the greatest questions, a skill of deflection. Great leaders have practiced this skill so often that it becomes part of their natural behaviour. The next time you are in a conversation, deflect the *flow*.

The Language of Deflection

The conscious effort required to practice deflection highlights the fact that none of us comes out of the womb 100% a team player. We have a nature that starts with self-preservation. Only through the discipline of deflection can we get our eyes off of us and pointed at what we might be able to do for others. Deflection is not only about pointing the conversation towards another person, but is embodied in the language we employ when describing our company, team, family and life. I have always chuckled a bit when people standing next to their wives unintentionally tell me a story about "my boy." *"Your* boy?" I think that it should have been *"our* boy." Those who are best at using the language of deflection create inclusive environments with their choice of words: Us instead of me; we instead of I; the team was amazing instead of *I was unbelievable!* The art of deflection is subtle, but when applied, it builds connection in the Team Game. When missing, it can erode relationships and a team's *hungry spirit*.

In fact, deflection is completely devoted to the team cause. It is John Wooden reminding his team to overtly share the credit, by asking his basketball players, after they scored a basket, "to always turn and point at the person that gave them the ball." The deflection connection amplifies a leader's integrity and influence throughout his or her team, just as it amplifies teammates' genuine care for one another.

Deflecting Accountability

Marc Crawford took over the coaching reins of the Vancouver Canucks during the 1998/1999 season. When they arrived, Marc and his Associate Coach, Mike Johnston observed a trend that they decided to change. In previous seasons the Canuck team had panicked with the puck in their own zone and, more often than not, their defensemen just fired it off the boards or glass into the neutral zone. In simple terms, when they finally had possession of the puck, players were not focused on keeping possession, but rather on getting it out of the zone! Marc and Mike believed this action did not optimize the strengths of the team. The Canucks had highly paid offensive forwards who were then forced to chase the puck, instead of carrying it, under this system. Therefore Marc and Mike made one change. Throughout the exhibition season they asked their defensemen never to put the puck off the boards, but always pass it tape to tape. In other words, the defensemen breaking out of their own zone had only one option, and that was to try to make a pass to another player on their team. You may be saying to yourself, "that doesn't seem very hard to do," but in fact, this was a huge change in the way this culture did business when under pressure.

Marc Crawford didn't stop there. He actually implemented what I call Deflecting Accountability. He assured his defensemen that if their attempt to pass was intercepted and their opponent scored, Marc would assume all responsibility. Crawford said, "If you do what I'm asking you to do and it goes wrong... I'll take the blame!"

Wow! That doesn't happen often in the NHL. When leaders find ways to mitigate their people's risk those people are more likely to take a crack at implementing the desired change. Removing the risk of retribution for wrong action is very effective in building *hungry* culture.

As I was writing this portion of the book and very focused on Deflecting Accountability as a *hungry* fuel type, I took a morning away from writing to meet with our financial planner, Dan Loney. He had a new product that he needed me to see before the end of the year. A feature of this product offering was the company's assurance that if I stayed with their investment instruments, they would guarantee a minimum 5% return, independent of financial market fluctuations. I realized right away that the company was using the principle of Deflecting Accountability. Find ways to deflect the risk and you will create *hungry* customers.

Deflecting Focus

"In the fall of 1843, a British novelist found himself facing financial uncertainty. Although his previous novels had sold

> "There is no limit to what can be accomplished if it doesn't matter who gets the credit."
> **Ralph Waldo Emerson**

moderately well, his family bills were mounting and the mortgage was due. One evening, while out for a walk along the Thames, he wandered into a rundown London neighbourhood. The streets were strewn with garbage, gutters overflowed with sewage, and pickpockets and streetwalkers were everywhere.

He thought back to his troubled childhood, when his father had been sent to debtors' prison, and how he himself had been forced to work at age 12, pasting labels on pots of boot polish for twelve hours a day, 6 days a week.

As he reached his home following his walk, he had a flash of inspiration. He thought of writing a Christmas story full of cheer and goodwill for people who, like he, had suffered poverty and had known what it was like to live in fear.

The question was whether, since it was only three months until Christmas, he could finish the book in time. He realized that it had to be a short book, not a full-length novel. He got right to work.

And before long, Charles Dickens had created *A Christmas Carol.*

Yet Dickens held to his original vision of making the book affordable for the widest possible audience, charging only five shillings a copy.

The response was overwhelming. The first 6,000 copies sold out by Christmas Eve. Today, Dickens' story is a literary classic.

Dickens said that writing that story transformed him. 'I was very much affected by that little book,' he later told a journalist, 'and quite reluctant to lay it aside even for a moment.'

Because of its low price, Dickens himself did not realize much profit from the sales of *A Christmas Carol.* It was, in a very real sense, a gift to the public.

By virtue of its popularity, however, the story created a much wider audience for Dickens' subsequent works.

His later novels, including *David Copperfield*, *A Tale of Two Cities*, and *Great Expectations*, all proved highly popular and financially profitable, and his place in literary history has been assured for all time."

Charles Dickens' fate changed when he deflected his intention! He removed his concern from his own woes and chose to find a way to brighten the lives of those less fortunate than he was. When we deflect our intention from personal gain to adding value to other people, amazing magic can happen. The magic strikes twice. While deflection adds value to the recipient, it accelerates the *hungry spirit* of the deflector.

Jay Abraham, a marketing genius, says, "The key to all life is value. Value is not what you get but what you give. It's figuring out what's important to other people, not just to you...It's pretty simple really, but we're so consumed about us, us, us. The real fast-track path to getting everything, anything, and more than everything that you want is putting others ahead of what you want and focusing on their needs, their wants, their desires, and fulfilling them." Deflecting your focus from what people can do for you to what you can do for them can be the missing glue that cements your relationships, the foundation that builds your team and gives you the business advantage over your competitors!

The same principle applies to professional speaking. My colleague, Vince Poscente, advised me that, "the single most important next step for most professional speakers is to change the emphasis of the talk from ME to YOU." In other words the subject of an accomplished speaker is the people who are listening, rather than the person who is speaking.

Scottish evangelist Henry Drummond said, "There are some men and women in whose company we are always at our best. While with them we cannot think mean thoughts or speak ungenerous words. Their mere presence is elevation to us. All the best stops in our nature are drawn out by our contact with them, and we find music in our soul that was never there before." As you continually point to others and not your own accomplishments, people will not only play for you, but go through the wall for you. It has been said that when you had dinner with William Gladstone, you left feeling that he was the wittiest, most brilliant, charming person on earth. But when you had dinner with Benjamin Disraeli, you left feeling that you were the wittiest, most brilliant, charming person on earth." The difference between these two British Prime Ministers was, in fact, Disraeli's practice of Deflecting.

Using a pen or pencil, shade in how full your Deflecting tank is today. How often do you focus on others?

Creating Collective Energy Exercise

Deflect your attention towards the "Rays" in your life.

1. For one day, find something or a number of things that you like, appreciate, or are thankful for, about each person you interact with.
2. Vocalize at least one of these appreciations in a direct conversation.
3. Deflect every conversation towards the other person.

Record your observations below.

_____

_____

_____

_____

_____

_____

After a day of deflecting, how did you feel? How did they feel?

_____

_____

_____

_____

_____

_____

Leadership Tips

1. Unless leaders learn the lesson of deflection early in their lives, they will never fully reach their potential. Monitor your conversations to discover how much they flow in the direction of deflection. People very seldom follow self-absorbed leaders.

2. A great way to deflect conversation is to ask questions. Make a habit of collecting questions that you can use to control conversation.

DEFLECTING
activates your COLLECTIVE TEAM ENERGY

Chapter

Hungry Influence:

Honouring

HUNGRY

Defining Honour

HONOUR:

1. To esteem
2. To exalt
3. To pay tribute to
4. To dignify
5. To keep a promise

Can you imagine the impact that these 5 actions might make in your home, workplace or team? Implementing the fuel of Honouring requires extra attention and a deliberate effort to change, but it is well worth it. Like Deflecting, the process of

Honouring takes the attention off of you and places it squarely on your people, energizing your *hungry* team.

Honouring Rules

Over a 25 year period, the Gallup organization compiled interviews with more than a million workers. Using data from these interviews, Marcus Buckingham and Curt Coffman demonstrated that the quality of the relationship between employees and their direct supervisors is the single most important variable in creating a healthy organizational culture. This relationship directly influences employee loyalty and productivity, for better or worse. More specifically, Buckingham and Coffman discovered that workers seek internal and emotional satisfaction from their supervisors, they want to know clearly what is expected of them and that they are valued, and they want a direct supervisor who encourages them to grow and develop. When such qualities are absent in a coach or manager employees begin to look elsewhere. In the words of Buckingham and Coffman, "People leave managers, not companies."

> "Trust men and they will be true to you; treat them greatly and they will show themselves great."
> **Ralph Waldo Emerson**

Following my last season playing professional hockey I was invited to interview with the Television Sports Network (TSN) to be a live analyst. For the next 12 seasons, I spent my winters talking on a number of television stations about the game I had played professionally for 15 seasons. During one of my last seasons in the industry I was the colour man for the Vancouver Canucks, broadcasting their game versus the Colorado Avalanche. This was, bar none, the most difficult broadcast that I ever worked. It was the game of the Todd Bertuzzi incident against Steve Moore.

During this very weird game all around, the Canucks found themselves down by 5 goals. The Vancouver Canucks finally managed to score two late goals, with long time fan-favourite Trevor Linden (my former roommate) tallying an assist on the second. This was significant because that single point pushed Linden into the number one position for points scored in Canuck history. The capacity crowd at General Motors Place (now Rogers Arena) recognized what was happening and began clapping for Linden, rising to their feet when Trevor returned to the ice four shifts later. In my role as a Colour Commentator I learned early that the "Colour" guy doesn't watch what everyone else watches, he or she needs to be on the lookout for other interesting parts of the game that people will want to know about. As Trevor Linden was acknowledging the crowd, my eyes locked on linesman Mike Cvik.

Mike Cvik was faced with an enormous Catch-22. Under today's NHL "hurry-up face-off" rules, Mike had 15 seconds to drop the puck. However, forcing the centreman to the dot and dropping the puck would totally shut down the standing ovation for Trevor. I was looking directly into big Mike's eyes, wondering what he was going to do. Eight, seven, six … it was evident that Mike had suddenly gotten an idea. Big Mike Cvik separated the two centremen, turned, and skated over towards the boards, promptly pretending to patch an invisible hole in the ice. His fellow-linesman, Lonny Cameron clued in to what Cvik was up to, skated to the scorekeeper's bench, grabbed a water bottle, and skated over to squirt water on the non-hole in the ice. With this charade, these two officials honoured Trevor Linden. They found a way to allow Trevor Linden to have a 1 minute and 15 second standing ovation instead of only 15 seconds. This was one of the greatest standing ovations that I have ever experienced, perhaps second only to the one I received when I played my 1000th NHL game.

I was struck by the two aspects of Honouring that I observed that night. Most people believe that Honouring only happens in front of a big crowd at a podium. In fact, Honouring very seldom happens there. The greatest potential for Honouring actually happens behind the scenes among our peers, in our daily grind. Secondly, opportunities to honour happen most often during our most difficult times.

Honouring is a powerful fuel that I watch for, but rarely put in my day-timer. It is a fuel that must be intentionally desired and developed, and I challenge myself and you to implement it more often. When honour is practiced in a culture, the Team Game is enriched.

The Foundation of Honour

The building blocks of Honouring have been undervalued. One stumbling block to sound relationships, according to The Arbinger Institute, is seeing people as **objects** instead of seeing people as **people**. Their finding has a direct correlation to what I call Honouring. The first thing to be conscious of in using this fuel is to guard against viewing people as objects. I was flying home with Jenni from a European speaking engagement when we found ourselves boarding a transfer bus that would take us from one terminal to another. Of course, everyone from the airplane was jamming into this small bus. Jenn found a seat and I stood. Noticing a lady standing nearby holding a young baby, Jenn immediately rose to give mother and baby her seat. Next to the aisle where I was standing, a woman was seated with her luggage, purse, passport and jacket piled on the seat next to her. She had obviously put all of these possessions on the seat beside her so that no one else could sit there. With this action she was selfishly viewing all of us standing in that bus as objects. We honour others when

> "For twenty years, my research has shown that the "views" that you adopt for yourself profoundly affects the way you lead your life. It can determine whether you become the person you want to be and whether you accomplish the things you value."
>
> **Carol Dweck Ph.D.**

we see them not as objects (to be used), but as created beings, as equals.

There is power in the reciprocal nature of Honouring. As you honour those around you, you will discover that those people tend to look for ways to reciprocate, because, as Psychologist Robert Cialdini has noted, the entire North American culture has totally bought into and feeds off the principle of reciprocity. If we do not pay attention and find ways to honour people, we will end up with a life where people will choose not to honour us, our company or our family. The obvious goal is not to abuse this knowledge, but rather to use it for the greater good, which in this case is to proactively create a culture of honour.

Here are two practical ways to honour those closest to you on a daily basis:

1. Value people's strengths above their weaknesses.
2. Honour people in the way you choose to resolve conflict.

Honouring Strengths

Discovering your people's strengths can be much more challenging than noticing their weaknesses, but it is vital. Gallup's Marcus Buckingham, who has started a crusade around strengths, sites that only 20% of American workers would actually say that they "play in their area of strength daily." I recently heard Buckingham give good advice in this area at a leadership summit. He articulated that strengths are not

> "What I found with the Celtics was a set of other players who were brilliant and accomplished. I needed to know who the different players were, what their tendencies were, their habits and their preferences. I had to learn about their thinking, their temperaments. For me to play my best game, I had to discover theirs."
>
> **Bill Russell**

necessarily what we are good at. Strengths are what we love to do. Buckingham advises discovering your strengths by recording your answer to the following three questions:

1. When you get up in the morning what can't you wait to get at?
2. When you look back on your day, about which parts or projects would you say, "That was really cool?"
3. What do you find you are doing when time stands still?

Here's the twist. I would like to challenge you to start observing how the people you interact with daily would answer these three questions. Let's get very practical here in a somewhat theoretical concept. You are Honouring your spouse, or best friend, or business colleague when you encourage them to live, as much as possible, in their areas of strength. When you discover what your spouse, or friend or colleague can't wait to get out of bed to do, when you track the times that they say "wow, that was cool" and "boy, time stood still today" and actually help them to do this more often, you are burning your Honouring fuel in high gear and refilling it at the same time.

Too many leaders fail to utilize this fuel, either completely taking it for granted, or refusing to believe in its power. Honouring is a noble concept which escalates as it reciprocates both positively and, unfortunately, negatively as well. If you fail to honour your teammates, at home or in the workplace, you run the risk of losing them.

Resolving Conflict

By definition conflict is a state of opposition or the clashing of opposed interests. Conflict can lead to productive and positive change or to the destruction and degradation of relationships and performance. When conflict is resolved in the spirit of Honouring, emphasis is placed on prioritizing the stability of the relationship.

> "Empathic listening gets inside another person's frame of reference. You look through it, you see the world the way they see the world, you understand their paradigm, you understand how they feel... you're listening to understand."
>
> **Stephen Covey**

While working for the RCMP in Vancouver, BC, Dr. Matt Logan was frequently called on to talk people down from suicide attempts. Matt worked tirelessly and effectively to engage distraught people in order to keep them safe from themselves. Matt faced high stakes conflict with every intervention.

Matt taught my Leadership cohort at Trinity Western University the simple acronym he developed for situations like these. Matt explained that this acronym was always in the back of his mind the entire time he was attempting to engage the distressed person. Matt's acronym, below, has been hugely instructive in my life as a leader.

V
A
L
U
E

V is to **Validate** the other person or the relationship. Matt would counsel to first look for common relational ground. When I asked Matt how he can relate to a person he has never met before, he had the perfect answer. Matt looks for connectors: "Hey, do you have a dog? Really? I have a dog! What's your dog's name?"

A is about **Asking**. I learned from Peter Drucker that in days of old we taught leaders how to tell, but in days of now we teach leaders how to ask. Questions allow us to gather further information, and resolution is not often reached in the absence of new information.

L reminds us to **Listen** to the answers. I happen to have been blessed and cursed with an active brain. As business colleagues are fully explaining a concept, my mind can often be already well down the road, wanting to jump forward. I am learning to listen. If necessary, I make a note of what my mind is racing toward, but then work to stay in the moment, actively listening. This brings me squarely back to the ingredient of Honouring. There may be no simpler and more powerful way to honour another human being, than to give them your undivided and fully present time.

U is for **Understanding** the other person's point of view before asking them to understand ours. By offering to understand a person's context, we proactively extend a large olive branch towards them. This presents the reciprocal opportunity to offer our perspective.

E brings us to the final step in conflict resolution. Both sides need to agree on **Empowered Action**. Without empowering movement away from the point of conflict, both sides stay stuck in a verbal quagmire. By agreeing to take this empowered action, both sides can move out of verbal conflict, and into shared solution.

Even though I have shared this VALUE acronym with many clients and teams, I am still amazed by its *value* proposition.

This is an amazingly practical process for honouring your people while you solve conflict. The value of VALUE lies in its clarity and simplicity.

There is a peripheral benefit to applying the VALUE module to other parts of your life. It works equally well in areas outside of conflict. I use this process daily to fill our company's sales funnel. I never just jump into the "ask." Begin by finding ways to develop or strengthen the relationship (**Validate**). If your client asks you an opening question, answer it politely, but don't use this "talking" opportunity to fill your client's ears with you. Instead, ask significant questions about his or her life (**Ask**). Build equity with your clients by actively listening to their answers (**Listen**). Unless you are speaking on the phone, of course, look them in the eyes, except where culture precludes, nod, and respond to their comments. Listening inside a sales opportunity relationship is a double edged sword, with both edges to your advantage. Engaged and active listening enhances your client's perception of being honoured, while giving you insight into your client's business pain, which your product or service can ease. Understanding (**Understand**) your client's point of view is critical to your sales process and bumping forward the next-steps (**Empowering Action**), keeps flow and professionalism in the relationship.

One of my clients in the construction industry recently applied VALUE to a difficult situation. This President had been dealing with a potential customer for a number of years, but they seemed to always butt heads and he never got the customer's business. After participating with his whole executive team in one of my interactive Leadership Training Sessions, he decided to apply the VALUE acronym to this potential customer. He later shared with me, "Ryan, instead of getting down to the point at hand, I paused and focused the conversation on the relationship. I then asked a number of important questions starting with: 'Do we have any outstanding issues that we should discuss?' That question opened up quite a dialogue that turned into a better understanding of how we should be positioning our services, and from there we landed the contract."

Honouring With our Words

"J.C. Penny, founder of the vast merchandizing chain, tells how he heard his father say on his deathbed, 'I know Jim will make it.' And from that time onward, Penny felt that he would succeed-somehow-although he had no tangible assets, no money, no education. Whenever he became discouraged, he would remember this prediction of his father's and he would "feel" that somehow he would make it, and make it he did.

> "Nothing is more honourable than a grateful heart."
>
> **Seneca**

Another man who had a history of failure told a counselor of overhearing an uncle say, 'Steve will never amount to anything; no one in the family ever has.' This subconscious feeling had blocked his path. So he replaced it with a goal and with the image of his accomplishment, and this chronic failure became a winner."

The most effective leaders in my life honoured their people by refraining from speaking negatively about them behind their backs. Anything instructive or constructive should be said to people and never *about* people. What we say about others always seems to get back to them.

The Highest Honour

While we honour others by the way we speak to and about them, the highest form of honour comes from the heart. A college professor instructed his sociology class to visit the worst slum area in Baltimore to obtain case histories of two hundred young boys. When the students returned, the professor asked them to record their prediction of each boy's future at the end of each case history. Without exception, the students wrote predictions like: "He hasn't got a chance."

Twenty-five years later another sociology professor came across the earlier study and decided to follow it up. Telling his class about the study, he asked his students to find out what had happened to the 200 boys. With the exception of 20 boys who had moved away or died, the students learned that 176 of the remaining 180 had achieved above average success as lawyers, doctors, and businessmen.

The professor was astounded and extremely curious to discover what had caused this unexpected result. He decided to pursue the study further. Fortunately, all of the men lived in Baltimore and he was able to interview each one. He asked them how they accounted for their success.

Each replied in an emotional voice that he owed his success to the same teacher. The University professor really wanted to discover the magic formula the teacher had used to pull those boys out of the slums. The teacher was also still living so he went to see her. When he asked the elderly, but still alert lady for her secret, the teacher's eyes sparkled and her lips broke into a gentle smile. "It's very simple," she answered, "I loved those boys."

Honouring Takes Courage

"Let me tell you about a young leader named Danny Rohrbough. Danny was fifteen years old, a high school freshman who loved computers, stereos, and big-screen TVs. He often helped out his dad in the family electronics business. He eagerly looked forward to getting his driver's permit.

On one warm spring day, Danny Rohrbough and more than four hundred of his fellow students were eating lunch in the high school cafeteria. Suddenly, the students were startled by the sound of gunfire just outside the building. Two male students in black trench coats were stalking the grounds, guns raised, firing at students. They killed a seventeen-year-old girl who was eating her lunch. Then they shot a young man sitting next to her eight times, leaving him alive but permanently paralyzed.

> "You can't treat a man like a butler and expect him to fight like a warrior."
>
> **General Tiny Freyberg**

The two killers then went down some stairs and entered the cafeteria. When the students in the cafeteria saw the armed boys, they fled. The killers tried to detonate some butane-powered bombs in the cafeteria, but they failed to explode. Danny Rohrbough was in the crowd of students who made it out of the cafeteria, running for safety. But unlike the other students, Danny stopped, went back, and held the door open so that his fellow students could get out of the cafeteria faster. He stood there holding the door until one of the two killers saw him, took aim, and shot him three times. Danny staggered a few steps down the walk, then stumbled and fell.

He died on the sidewalk, just a few steps from safety. The gunfire and screams continued. The gunmen killed twelve students and a teacher that day. It was Tuesday, April 20, 1999, and the school was Columbine High School in Littleton, Colorado."

Most of us in our lifetime will not be asked to honour people by putting our lives on the line. Danny would have been justified had he chosen to run clear of this great tragedy… others did. Instead, Danny chose to honour his fellow students when he held that door open and we honour his name by remembering his courage.

Honourable Motive

Honour is most effective when it comes from a pure motive.

"One rainy afternoon an elderly lady walked into a Philadelphia department store. Most clerks ignored her but one solicitous young man asked if he could help her. When she replied that she was just waiting for the rain to end he didn't try to sell her something she didn't want and he didn't turn his back. Instead he brought her a chair. When the rain let up she thanked the young man and asked for his card. A few months passed. The owner of the store received a letter asking that this young man be sent to Scotland to take orders for furnishing an entire castle!

The letter writer was the elderly lady for whom the clerk had provided the chair. She happened to be Andrew Carnegie's mother. By the time he packed his bags to leave for Scotland the young clerk was a partner in the department store."

Author Unknown

When I was playing for the Montreal Canadiens during the early '80's, our team found itself in Boston Garden to play the Bruins for our final game of the season. The kicker was that we already knew we would be playing these same Bruins in the first round of the playoffs. You can imagine how that game went. The Bruins were trying to send a message and we were trying not to hear it.

What a rough game it turned out to be. During the first period I ended up in a big scrap. The same thing came my way in the second period. In the third period my shoulder was shoved by a Bruins player and by accident my stick swung around and hit Terry O`Reilly on the top of the head. He wasn't wearing a helmet. I looked at Terry and said, "It was a total accident!" He looked at me and said, "I don't care… we have to go!"

We scrapped for a bit and then both fell. I quickly realized that there was something wrong with this situation: I was on top. It felt like I was going to get the upper hand in this fight because all of a sudden he wasn't moving. "Taz" looked up at me as I was going to land one and said, "My shoulder's out." I said, "No problem," and got off. I always had a strong sense that he would have done the same for me.

Some time later I got a call from Nate Greenberg, the P.R. director of the Boston Bruins. I was thinking what's going on here? Did the Canadiens trade me to Boston and forget to tell me? Nate assured me that all was fine, then added, "We have two tickets waiting at the airport for you and your wife. We have cleared this with your GM, Serge Savard and your coach; you are coming to Boston Friday night. Terry O'Reilly is having his retirement banquet that night and he wants you to come as the only non-Bruin."

He remembered! Honour begets honour.

Using a pen or pencil, shade in how full your Honouring tank is today. How often do you honour others?

Letters of Honour Exercise

Let me recommend a life-changing action to finish off our chapter on Honouring. This is inspired by the movie *PS I love You*. In this world of Internet, e-mail, cell phones, and instant access, the letter has become the jewel of the heart. Choose 5 people that you want to honour this week and send them each a letter by snail mail.

Name of person:_____

How will I honour them in my letter?

_____

_____

Name of person:_____

How will I honour them in my letter?

_____

_____

Name of person:_____

How will I honour them in my letter?

_____

_____

Name of person:_____

How will I honour them in my letter?

_____

_____

Name of person:_____

How will I honour them in my letter?

_____

_____

Leadership Tips

1. Mac Anderson says, "A service culture doesn't just happen by accident. The company is always a reflection of the person at the helm. Their attitude, their values, and their commitment to service excellence will drive the actions of others in the organization. Always has... always will." When you focus on finding ways to honour your people, your culture will find ways to make Honouring a priority.

2. Leaders honour people in many ways, from the way they speak about them when they are not present to the way they treat their children and families. If you want to honour me, honour our children. As part of Honouring your people, honour their children.

Chapter

Hungry Relationships:

Connecting

HUNGRY

The Problem with Perception

During my time with the Montreal Canadiens, I was fortunate to experience two amazing journeys to the Stanley Cup final. As I explained near the beginning of the book, the first culminated in a 1986 Stanley Cup victory for our team, but the second trip saw us lose to the Calgary Flames in 1989. Both journeys were exhilarating, but obviously the '89 loss was hugely disappointing. After that run to the final, the Canadiens, like many teams during that NHL time period, felt that they needed to become younger and began a program of *change*. Consequently, for the first time in my career I found myself downsized. I played less, I played a lesser role on the team, and in the first game of the first round of the playoffs that season my coach, Pat Burns, who sadly passed away in November 2010, actually didn't even dress me. Talk about disappointment; talk about being angry. I'm good enough to help the team get to the Cup final one season, but not good enough to play in the playoffs the next. During this experience I had a dilemma as a player. All my life I had played team sports, and had always relayed to everyone in the game that I was a team player. Now I had to live up to those words.

> "The problem with communication is the illusion that it has been accomplished."
> **George Bernard Shaw**

In the NHL, if you are not dressing for the game, you do two things: you support the players who are playing by patting every one on the backside, and then you get out of the way. It's their game. So I supported the guys and stayed out of the way and our team lost game one. What a weird feeling in my gut: "Oh darn we lost... oh, we *lost*!!!" I was upset that our team lost, but anxious to see whether this loss might get selfish little me back into the lineup next game. Either way, I sensed that the players and coaching staff were in no mood to chat, so again, getting out of the way, I headed to the team bus which was parked behind Boston Garden.

On my way to the bus a young man stopped me. His name was Billy and he was a huge Ryan Walter fan. I had met Billy years ago after a Bruins game. On this occasion I could sense that Billy was visibly upset. He grabbed my attention and started in on my coach, Pat Burns. "How could Burns not play you in game one? That's why the team lost! You are the best player on the team! You are going to be an all-star..."

I'm thinking to myself, "boy does this feel good–bring it on Billy boy." After letting Billy rant on for a while I said, "No problem buddy, we'll beat the "Bs" on Tuesday and all will be good."

I said my goodbyes to Billy and jumped on the bus, where there were only 2 people, the bus driver and me. The third person to board the bus was Pat Burns and as he stepped on, he yelled to the back of the bus, "That's all I needed, Wally!" On our team, my nick-name was Wally. Now, what had I done? I had been the perfect team player! I had patted everyone on the backside and gotten out of the way. My overactive brain, trying to understand what was happening, wondered if maybe Pat Burns walked to the bus by the same route that I did and my buddy Billy had given him an ear-full for not dressing me? THAT A BOY, BILLY!

Now, at least in my mind, I had a serious problem. I was thinking that the man most in control of my NHL career hated my guts. Over the course of that career I have fought many tough players (I'm not sure if that was courage or sheer stupidity), so why was I afraid to communicate with my boss? I mustered up the courage, and as our team was boarding the airplane back to Montreal, I stopped everyone in order to ask Pat Burns, "Burnsie, is there anything wrong between you and me?" I hated the way those words came out! Why is it that when we speak to our boss, we "squeak?"

Anyway, Pat responded with a puzzled, "No."

Now I was the puzzled one. I asked again, "But when you stepped on the bus at Boston Garden you screamed out, "That's all I needed Wally!"

Pat replied, "Ryan, it wasn't about you. The refereeing in that game was horse-bleep and the chief of referees, Wally *Harris*, was walking by the door of the bus just at that time."

Wow, what a strange feeling I had in my gut. It wasn't even about me, and yet my perception of this situation had caused me to feel and believe that in reality, it was. Here's what haunts me: what if I had not mustered the courage to clarify what Pat Burns was saying, to really understand what he meant? Think of the agony that I would have endured worrying all summer. Our perception of any given situation is, at that point, our reality.

I once heard a story of a young single mom doing her best to raise two teenage boys. She was caught in that difficult period where the boys were testing her will, and she happened to tell the next door neighbour about the difficulty she was having. The neighbour said, "Oh, don't be too upset. We went through that when our boys were teenagers too. We ended up taking our boys to the local priest and he really straightened them out."

"Really?" said the young single mom. "I'll make an appointment right away."

> "Communication is based on the same root as communion, which denotes an intense, two-way sharing or exchange - a coming together of thoughts and ideas. Real communication has to do with careful listening, observation, and dialogue…"
> **Fredrick Reichheld**

So the young single mom dropped her two boys off at the local priest's office the next day. The priest brought the older boy, Johnny, into his office and asked the younger boy, Jimmy, to stay in the waiting room. The priest was silent for awhile and then looked directly at the boy and asked, "Johnny, where is God?" Johnny was caught off guard with this line of questioning and didn't know how to respond. The priest asked again, "Johnny where is God?" Johnny was starting to get flustered now and again stayed silent. The priest with a little more authority asked for the third time, "Johnny, where is God?"

As soon as that question popped out of the priest's mouth, Johnny bolted out of the office, grabbed Jimmy, and while running out of the church said, "Jimmy we've got to get out of here. They've lost God and they're trying to pin it on us."

Ronald Reagan had a favorite story about a young newspaper photographer in the LA area who was sent on assignment to get aerial photos of a large fire not far from the city. His boss told him to get to the local airport as soon as he could where a small plane would be waiting for him. He hurried off to the airport and hopped on the small plane with a young pilot. They took off and the newspaper photographer pulled out his large camera and asked the pilot to veer over towards the fire so that he could get the photos that he needed. With this new information, the young pilot, with a frightened look on his face said, "You mean you aren't the flight instructor?" Assumptions can lead to dangerous outcomes.

These stories illuminate the potential problems inherent in misperception. Our minds not only misinterpret what is said incorrectly, but they often imagine options about what might happen next and create wrong next steps. Wrong perception often precipitates wrong action. The central issue in the preceding scenarios gone wrong is the receiver of the information not understanding its intent.

Connecting, not Communicating

In this age of capital "C" communication, we often don't! Here is the fundamental problem: we confuse the sending of information with actual communicating. Often in the corporate and sports world we see communicating as: "Sit down and listen up; I want to communicate to you." A key component to sustaining the *hungry spirit* personally and culturally is to recognize that communication is not enough; true connection must take place.

I prefer the concept of *Connecting* to the word communicating. Communication, in our culture, is fraught with the stigma that we are *delivering* information. We are *sending* an email. We are *letting people know* what we need them to know. The next step beyond sending is Connecting! Connection brings a sense of two-way flow, an interchange of ideas with successful contact.

Defining Connection:

1. to link two things
2. to associate somebody or something with another
3. to get along well
4. to establish telecommunication link between people

Connection differs fundamentally from communication in a number of ways. One difference is highlighted by the image of *sparks*. When two electrical lines, one positive and one negative, connect, sparks are created, followed by a powerful flow of energy if the connection is continued. In today's world there may be a perception of communication, when in fact the people involved are often passive to the point that there is no connection whatsoever. For true connection to happen, there must be an initial interest by all parties, at the very least.

> "They may forget what you said, they may forget what you did, but they will never forget how you made them feel."
>
> **Carl W. Buechnew**

While communication often gets confused with the distribution of information, much like a newspaper offering information without dialogue, connection creates energy of motion. Interactive, web-based media has recognized the need for, and power of, two-way connection over the old one-way delivery of information. *Hungry* teams use dialogue instead of monologue.

The five dysfunctions of teams, as noted by Lencioni in *The Five Dysfunctions of Team*, inattention to results, avoidance of accountability, lack of commitment, fear of conflict, and absence of trust could all be overcome with a large dose of creative connection, in my opinion. From my observation of corporate and sports dressing rooms, I have come to believe that most cultures fall away from the *Hungry* zone and into ambivalence because leaders mistakenly thought that connection was happening on the team. Executives tell us that 86% of their success or failure as a manager depends on how well they connect with their people.

Obviously connection only occurs when someone understands you - not simply when you speak. In other words, we shouldn't mistake speaking for true connection. Words are merely the tip of the iceberg. They are what the world gets to see. What it doesn't get to see is the intent, the thinking that lies below the surface, and this is where meaning gets messed up. To enhance the *hungry spirit*, communication is out and Connecting is in.

Giving Permission

A study on firefighters by researchers Wendy Joung, Beryl Hesketh, and Andrew Neal found that granting upfront permission was critical for creating a culture of Connecting. They discovered that: "Team communication could be vastly enhanced by an up-front team brain-storming and collaborating session to generate ideas about how communication might go wrong and what the fixes for this might be. This creates a platform to give everyone permission to try the new techniques, potentially mess up, and then try again. This makes the ideas and solutions explicit and connecting instead of disconnecting the team."

I have found in my work with corporate clients, organizations and sports teams that giving permission is extremely important and often taken for granted. The enemy of permission is assumption. There is a tendency, over time, for leaders to assume that they still have permission to speak

> "Eighty-five percent of the reason you get a job, keep that job, and move ahead in that job has to do with your people skills and people knowledge."
>
> **Cavett Robert**

their minds and their peace, rather like the husband who says, "Listen I told you 20 years ago when I married you that 'I love you,' and if anything changes I'll let you know." Leaders and their people must check in to make asking permission part of their Team Connection Solution, so they are on-the-table explicit rather than under-the-rug implicit.

During my time as a coach in the NHL I was asked to spend extra time personally mentoring a number of our players. One young player was really struggling and on the edge of being sent down to our farm team. I was specifically instructed to "get that player turned around." I began my conversation with this young player by setting parameters that we both could work within. We agreed on and described where his game was at that time (not great), and then what his game needed to look like for us to win a Stanley Cup.

I then did something that seemed to make all of the difference. I asked his permission to coach his very best. Asking permission moved us out of Boss/Employee mode and into a Mentor/Protégé relationship. Together we created clarity around what I expected from him and what it looked like when he delivered. He gave me permission to hold him accountable to the things he agreed to do. When he performed the way we had agreed, I was in his face: "That's exactly what we need – nice!" When he failed to do what we had agreed upon, I was in his face: "Remember, we said that's not going to work." Asking permission completed the process that helped this player not only turn around, but excel.

It is never a surprise to me that *hungry* teams have leaders who take strong initiative in team connection. If leaders fail to initiate a strong culture of permission, they run the risk of creating a disconnected team. Opening team dialogue around granting permission to connect would be a brilliant step in assuring that your team sustains its *hungry* spirit.

Improve Connection with Carriers

I am thankful to have the exciting advantage of a direct connection to many amazing people in professional sports. NHL coach Dave King talked to me about a concept that he developed late in his professional coaching career. He calls it *carriers*: "I have coached for a long time, and I have always seen two categories of players: there are carriers and there are guys who have to be carried. I have always tried to surround myself with more carriers. I have gone back and looked at all my team pictures and asked, 'Why is this team better than that team?' Usually I realize I had more carriers that year, more guys who could carry other people, who had more natural energy, who had more natural courage, and that's why they competed the way they competed; that's why they influenced the rest of the group. If you have too many guys who need to be carried, you are in for a long darn season."

> "In everyone's life, at some time, our inner fire goes out. It is then burst into flame by an encounter with another human being. We should all be thankful for those people who rekindle the inner spirit."
>
> **Albert Schweitzer**

Dave King then explained to me how he uses this *carrier* concept to make sure the messages to his players stick. Dave and his coaching staff first identify which 5 or 6 players have the most influence throughout the team. These would be the captains, obviously, but potentially also a back-up goalie or a 4th line forward. He then brings these *carriers* into his coaching room at different points during the season to get their feedback around what kind of message it would be appropriate for him to deliver. King then gets his whole team together and delivers the message. Dave King says that a leader is most vulnerable when he or she has just delivered the message, turns, and walks out of the room. At that point what happens in the room amongst the team is reality. King maintains that many messages delivered by a leader fall flat on the floor. But King doesn't worry about that happening, because if the message falls flat on the floor, the *carriers* sitting in the room pick the message up and make it stick. The *carriers* deliver the message firstly because it originated with them, and secondly, because they have the intimate connection with teammates to make sure the message is not just heard, but understood.

There is a Time to Disconnect

Up to this point I have been celebrating the importance of relational connection and the positive influence it can bring. Just before my fourth NHL training camp with the Washington Capitals I received a phone call at 7am from our new General Manager, David Poile, saying, "Good morning Ryan. I've traded you." I was the captain of the Capitals at that time and the shock of this news made the rest of the conversation fade and blur. Trades are never easy and they are the hardest of all on wives and families. I was traded with Rick Green from the Washington Capitals for 4 Montreal Canadiens players in a blockbuster move. Rick and I were flown into Montreal on the day of the trade to begin training camp with the Canadiens. As we walked through what was then Dorval Airport, we picked up the *Montreal Gazette* newspaper. There in bold type on the front page of the Sports section the headline read: **WORST TRADE IN NHL HISTORY**. Apparently we were the worst part. I internalized those words and the city's expectations of me throughout that training camp and remember its start as one of my most difficult. Rick and I were vindicated in 1986 when we won a Cup, but it took time to shed that headline.

> "The inability to forget is far more devastating than the inability to remember."
>
> **Mark Twain**

There are times in our lives when we should never allow words and messages to connect with us. This was one of those times. It is important to filter what other people say about us. If someone calls you a loser, it's still up to you whether to believe what they say or not. Connecting has a give and take element to it; sometimes we shouldn't take.

Connect with a Story

In his farewell address on Jan. 11, 1989, US President Ronald Reagan said, "I won a nickname: 'The Great Communicator.' But I never thought it was my style or the words I used that made a difference. It was the content. I wasn't a great communicator, but I communicated great things." When he was running for president, Ronald Reagan verbally painted a picture of a national renewal, a "Morning in America." Many voters bought into Reagan's strategic story and elected him president in a landslide. In his inaugural address, Reagan made sure that Congress, the next audience whose buy-in he needed, heard his story loud and clear. "It is time to reawaken this industrial giant," Reagan declared, "to get government back within its means, and to lighten our punitive tax burden. And on these principles, there will be no compromise." Reagan's "Morning in America" story was so compelling and projected such a positive future for the country that it was difficult, even for his political opponents, not to buy in.

Cultures are created by significant stories. "History, in its broadest sense, is the story of humanity's past." The power of the story has also shaped my own life. If I have done one thing right, it is that I have listened to, collected, and shared stories. Most people do the first, but very few people have disciplined themselves to do the second in order to be able to do the third.

After I played 15 seasons of professional hockey, I spent 15 more coaching our three sons in minor hockey. Without exception, I always started every pre-game speech with a significant story. I found that the story focused the players minds and captured their hearts. Touching both the Heart Side and the Smart Side, the right story, well-told, prepared each of them to play their Best

Game! The story pointed to a principle, not necessarily connected to sport, but always connected to the game of life. The players remembered the stories I told, long after they had forgotten the wins and losses. What amazes me is that these stories now have the same effect on adults.

Whether I am speaking to 6 or 600 people, these same stories, and those I have since added, can generate minutes of complete silence followed by roars of laughter. Stories hit each of us differently, just where we need them most. The vast majority of the stories I share come from my personal experience. Sharing them allows me to add value to others. Had I not recorded them early, most of them would be long forgotten, and void of any potential to encourage someone else.

Monologue is one-way communication, intended to inform. Dialogue is two-way conversation, intended to include. Connecting is mutual interaction, intended to ignite. In fact, Connecting is the fuel with the greatest potential for powering your *hungry* team.

Using a pen or pencil, shade in how full your Connecting tank is today. How strong are your connections?

Connecting Exercise

A farmer went into his attorney's office wanting to file for divorce from his wife. The attorney asked, "May I help you?" to which the farmer replied, "Yeah, I want to get one of those *dayvorces*."

The attorney asked, "Well, do you have any grounds?" and the farmer answered, "Yeah, I got about 140 acres."

The attorney said, "No, you don't understand. Do you have a Case?" and the farmer replied, "No, I don't have a Case, but I have a John Deere."

The attorney said, "No, you really don't understand. I mean, do you have a grudge?"

And the farmer replied, "Yeah, I got a grudge. That's where I park my John Deere."

The attorney, still trying, asked, "No sir, I mean do you have a suit?"

The farmer replied, "Yes, sir, I got a suit. I wear it to church on Sundays."

The exasperated and frustrated attorney said, "Well, sir, does your wife beat you up or anything?"

The farmer replied, "No sir. We both get up about 4:30."

Finally, the attorney said, "Okay. Let me put it this way. WHY DO YOU WANT A DIVORCE?"

And the farmer answered, "Well, I can never have a meaningful conversation with her."

Author Unknown

List three people you need to have a meaningful connection with. Creating these connections will clarify the relationship to help you both stay *hungry*.

1. _____

2. _____

3. _____

Prioritize and Connect!

Leadership Tips

1. 86% of a leader's perceived ability to lead comes from his or her capacity to connect. This means that money can be very well spent on a personal coach to help you hone that skill. If you decide not to hire a coach, I would recommend that you accept every available opportunity to practice speaking publicly.

2. Generation Y members of the workforce notice who leaders are and what leaders do, well before leaders open their mouths. *Being* a great leader first will help to ensure that your people actually hear your message.

TEAM GAME ACTION SUMMARY

RELATIONAL FUEL

Deflecting: activates your COLLECTIVE TEAM ENERGY

Honouring: activates your TEAM INFLUENCE

Connecting: activates your RELATIONAL CLARITY

The final 3 Fuel types place emphasis on how we interact with people next to us. All of us play on multiple teams. Our teammates have huge influence on our personal *hungry spirit* and vice versa. Practice **Deflecting** to be a positive force on a great team. **Honouring** provides relational glue. As you honour people (especially behind their backs) you influence your culture to switch from me to us. **Connecting** keeps your teams functioning at a high level. As you have "great" conversations to sustain clarity, you will be a great team.

As you read through the Team Game section, I asked you to record some of your thoughts and ideas to make each Relational Fuel concept more personal to you. If you are having trouble writing in the book then I highly recommend that you purchase the companion handbook so you can more easily work through these powerful exercises (www.hungryfuellingyourbestgame. com/handbook). My desired goal is that you personalize the application of these principles and incrementally increase your performance because you did.

Each of these 3 Relational Fuels is critical and warrants your attention. At the end of each chapter you have the opportunity to fill in your personal fuel gauge for each fuel type. How full are your Deflecting, Honouring, and Connecting tanks? In other words, how fully is each fuel type working to bring optimal health to your *hungry spirit*?

FREE GIFT!

For extra OUTER GAME development, go online to our readers-only exclusive page:

www.hungryfuellingyourbestgame.com/teamgame
password: teamgame

11

Chapter

Hungry to be My Best:
Game On

HUNGRY

Why Not?

Do you remember the Rock and Roll Hall of Fame worker I told you about near the beginning of the book? He existed to exit; he couldn't wait to leave. Even if he had chosen his job purely out of financial necessity, he still had a choice, and he chose Ambivalence. That is not what I want for you or me.

Remember the premise of why:

1. The health of your *hungry spirit* is directly connected to your quality of life.
2. Sustaining your *hungry spirit* is directly connected to your personal performance.

Throughout my lifetime I have often asked myself a simple question to help me stay *hungry*: **Why not?** Why not play on a winning team? Why not develop an amazing culture? Why not create an incredible family? Why not push to play your Best Game? **Why not live *hungry*?**

Snap Shot

I want you to have a quick, clear picture of the health of your *hungry spirit*. To create substantial change you must start with an honest gut-feel for where you are right now. You will find an overview below of each fuel type and its corresponding action to assist you in completing your *hungry* dashboard which follows:

Fuel	Action
Purpose & Passion	Activates your Hungry CORE
Futuring	Activates your DESIRE to PURSUE
Believing	Activates your WILL to WIN
Framing	Activates your PRIORITY of ACTION
Constructing	Activates your PERFORMANCE ENVIRONMENT
Rebounding	Activates your RECOMMITMENT
Deflecting	Activates your COLLECTIVE TEAM ENERGY
Honouring	Activates your TEAM INFLUENCE
Connecting	Activates your RELATIONAL CLARITY

Your Hungry Dashboard

Your Hungry Dashboard has 9 fuel gauges which you can fill in or copy from the end of each chapter for a snap shot measurement of the state of your INNER game, OUTER game and TEAM game. Make use of the dashboard as a great tool to monitor your personal fuel levels or those of your team. Keep your tanks full to stay *hungry*.

Small Adjustments Have Big Impact

The events of 9/11 impacted the world. They also impacted me personally on a number of levels because I'm constantly in the air. Less than one year after that terrible tragedy I flew into Washington DC's Reagan National Airport. I had flown the same route hundreds of times in the past, but this flight was different. All was relatively smooth until about 40 minutes before we were to land in the Nation's Capital. The pilot's voice came over the intercom with the instruction that if anyone needed to use the restroom or stretch, then they should do it now because the crew had been instructed "to implement the following *new rules*: 30 minutes outside of Reagan Airport everyone must remain seated until the plane has landed. If anyone even stands up during the final 30 minutes of today's flight, the pilots and crew are under strict orders to turn the plane around and land in Ohio." With this one small adjustment in the landing procedure at Reagan National Airport, the airline industry had significantly reduced the chances of terrorists replicating the 9/11 tragedy.

Small adjustments consistently implemented over time have a significant effect! Ray Kroc, the founder of Macdonald's increased his sales by more than 30% just by saying, "'Would you like fries with that?" Making small behavioral adjustments to tune up your personal and cultural *hungry spirit* gives you a better chance of achieving the success you are pursuing. I urge you to keep on steadily adjusting your 9 fuel gauges upward, a little at a time.

Increase your Spark

Blogger Dayna Steelet's unnamed brother-in-law calls it a spark. I call it the *hungry spirit*.

"I spent Thanksgiving week in New York City with family including my brother-in-law who just opened a 5-star boutique hotel in the heart of SoHo. Not only is it a beautiful hotel with amazing customer service but it is also a company that firmly believes in taking care of their employees as well. In other words, the kind of company we all want to work for.

Heading out to dinner one night, we passed a doorman from a competing hotel flagging a cab for a customer. Unnamed brother-in-law casually asked him who he worked for. With a surly expression, not a smile to be found, he snarled '(insert big chain name here).'

Undeterred, unnamed brother-in-law went on to ask, 'Do you like working there?' Surly doorman snapped back, 'Yeah, it's ok.' Still not a smile or kind word to be found. As we continued on our dinner journey, I asked unnamed brother-in-law if he was in the habit of stealing hotel employees off the streets of New York City.

He simply replied, 'I'm looking for a spark.' He went on to explain that he has already hired people he has met along the way, some with even NO hotel experience, to work in customer service positions including the phones, front desk, housekeeping, and doormen **because** they had a spark."

Although we may not find ourselves receiving on the spot job offers, as we fill up our 9 fuel tanks, we increase the "spark" that makes our life exciting. That excitement for life and jump in our step is the Outer Game result of Inner Game growth. General George Patton said, "The fixed determination to have acquired the warrior soul, to either conquer or perish with honour, is the secret to victory." Multiply that warrior soul/hungry spirit and you can achieve victory in your Team Game.

Action!

When Vasco da Gama made his triumphant voyage around the Cape of Good Hope he took 160 men with him, but returned with only 60. It is easy to speculate that so many perished because of pirate attacks or fierce storms, but all 100 sailors actually died of scurvy. In 1601 the English sea captain, John Lancaster discovered a cure for scurvy. Lancaster gave his sailors lime juice every day, and every sailor who didn't die by drowning, or at the hand of a pirate, returned safely home. Even though Lancaster discovered the information to save the lives of countless sailors, it took nearly 200 years for the rest of the world to catch on. In fact, the British were initially mocked for this practice, and nicknamed "limeys." The method for saving lives was available, but for the next 200 years far too many sea captains and ship doctors failed to act upon it. **They knew it, but died because they didn't** *do it!*

> "I don't believe in a fate that falls on us no matter what we do. I do believe in a fate that will fall on us if we do nothing."
> **Ronald Reagan**

From Practice to Playing

I have provided enough information, enough pondering, enough process, enough practicing!

> "The way to get started is to quit talking and begin doing."
> **Walt Disney**

Professional athletes are wise to understand that the *practice* mindset is left brain and analytical. It is the thought process on steroids. The *playing* mindset is free flowing, fun, and in-the-zone reactive. Unfortunately, our educational system teaches us to be in the *practice* mindset most of the time.

When I played my second round of golf last summer, I had

what I call *second game expectations*. With the expectation that I should be much better than I demonstrated in my first game, I was thinking instead of just *playing*. My mind was focused on analysing my hand-grip, feet-positioning, weight-transfer... That whole open-loop process of going through the steps was a thinking traffic jam that simply hijacked my performance.

The opposite of that golf game would be a round of golf played by a professional golfer. A golf pro is loose, reactive, focused; everything just flows. Here's the key. Use the *practice* mindset to prepare for performing but the *playing* mindset when the game's on the line. Don't merge the two concepts; separate them.

Unfortunately, our brain can force us back into the *practice* mindset during performance. If I asked you to run along an eight inch-wide piece of steel lying on the ground, could you do it? Of course you could, in a heartbeat. But if I were to raise the same piece of steel twenty feet off the ground and asked you to run across it in the same way, what would happen? You would process the consequences, the height, and the risk, and certainly slow down your progress. Good idea.

The problem is that when the game is on the line and perform-ance counts, if you follow the practice mindset your tendency is to be more careful, more critical of the process, and more focused on what you are supposed to do, instead of just doing it. This is often the reason that even professional athletes' performances are sometimes reduced. They are over-analyzing the process of how they are supposed to play, instead of staying in the more reactive, playing mindset zone.

When I tried to analyse all of the components of my golf swing while playing, I created over-tension which inhibited my fluidity of motion and reactive thought process. While reading this book you have taken in a great amount of information. My concern now is that you may stay in the *practice* mindset, processing, instead of flowing into the *playing* mindset with a few desired changes. Thinking through the process is good for practicing but not for *playing*! When preparing for the sales call or an athletic competition it's good to be in the *practice* mindset. Preparation is about being process-driven. But when the sales call is on or it's game time, we have to be smack in the middle, flowing, reacting, and *playing*. In essence our preparation is done; now we react and enjoy and perform.

I personally learned this lesson as a professional athlete and then again as a professional speaker and trainer. During the early years of my speaking career I didn't want to miss a single opportunity to add value to my clients so I had piles of notes that I would drag up to the podium. A speaker who reads notes from the podium, not wanting to miss any points, is entrenched in a *practice* mindset. A speaker who is prepared and rehearsed, with no notes, is flowing from a *playing* mindset. With the need to stay *hungry* firmly entrenched in the peripheral parts of your mind, it's time to get back to *playing* your game.

Time to Play

I love the lingo of professional sport. One particular phrase meant more than anything else if a fellow teammate said it about me. The statement was simply: "**He comes to play**." This meant that I was on my game, competed hard, and had impact every night.

I played all 15 of my NHL seasons against arguably the best hockey player in history, Wayne Gretzky. Wayne's scoring records speak for themselves and his awards and trophies will undoubtedly hang in the Hockey Hall of Fame forever. But the thing that I admired about Wayne had less to do with records or trophies, and more to do with how he acquired them. Wayne *came to play every night*. It has been said that the difference between an amateur and a professional is that while the amateur only performs when he or she feels like it, the professional *shows up* for every event. You can't show up if you aren't *hungry*.

I'm Hungry

At the beginning of this book I used our team's 1986 Stanley Cup victory to introduce you to what I call the *Hungry spirit*. What you may not know about the 1986 Stanley Cup run was that I *missed it*; I missed the entire run up to the Stanley Cup final.

With 3 games to go in the 1985-86 regular season, I broke my ankle. Our team doctor cast my right foot and told me to enjoy watching the playoffs. I watched the momentum off the first round victory over the Boston Bruins propel our Montreal Canadiens players to a higher level.

For the first ten days after breaking my ankle and not being able to play in the playoffs, I was a bitter puppy. My mind dwelt on: "What if my team goes to the final and I miss my only opportunity to win a Stanley Cup?" I was no fun to be around. My sulking attitude caused me to spiral down into a frustrated, and intermittently ambivalent state.

On day 11 I decided to change. My perspective changed suddenly because I revitalized my Inner Game. Instead of

> "We are all, right now, living the life that we choose."
> **Peter McWilliams**

focusing on what might happen without me, which was outside of my control, I began to think about what I *could* control. I reignited the **Passion** I had lost when my ankle broke and used the skill of **Futuring** by creating a simple and clear vision: if my team arrives in the Stanley Cup final, then I'll be there too. I challenged myself into **Believing** that it could actually happen. Every day, instead of sulking and asking, "Why me," I chose instead to ask, "Why not?"

The changes in my Inner Game started to rapidly force change in my Outer Game. I began **Framing** in the actions that would prepare me physically to be my best and **Framing** out distractions like negative thinking. Instead of watching the playoff games from row 10, seat 23 while eating the famed Montreal Forum chiens chauds avec moutarde, I began to watch every game on TV in the dressing room while working out. Lifting weights was easy, but I had a broken ankle. How was I going to stay in aerobic shape to compete in the final? When you are *hungry*, you find a way. I took a stationary bike, turned it upside down, hockey-taped it to a table and rode the bike with my arms. (My pipes were huge; I looked like Popeye!) I could have trained alone, but I realize I was unconsciously **Constructing** a rehabilitation environment that kept me close to my teammates and surrounded by the playoff presence of the Montreal Canadiens. I continually chose **Rebounding** over self-pity. The combination of fuel I was burning, everything I needed to rev up my Inner and Outer Games strengthened my will to rebound, which was vital, because our team continued to win without me.

As a result my Team Game caught fire. I practiced **Deflecting** any attention that came my way to the players who were actually playing the game and **Honouring** the stakeholders around our team by choosing to have an upbeat attitude. Our personal energy is amazingly revitalized when we get our focus off of "poor me" and onto "how can I add value to the people around me?" **Connecting** with the players, doctors, trainers and coaching staff was critical for me to stay in the loop and to remain an integral part of the team. I find that when things are difficult in our lives there is a tendency to retreat and not connect with the people who can help us climb out of our hole. I chose to fuel-up instead of powering-down.

Finally, it happened! My team arrived! Two days before the first game of the final round of the Stanley Cup playoffs, my friend, Montreal Canadiens' orthopaedic surgeon Eric Lenzcner, asked me to come up to his office so he could take a look at how my ankle was doing. Eric took some pictures and while acknowledging that the fracture wasn't completely healed, he then added, "Do you want to give it a try?"

I answered, "Eric, you'd let me?"

Dr. Lenzcner told me, "I've been watching you work out; you're in great shape; let's see if that ankle holds up." Eric added a little freezing before games and our trainer, Gataen Lefebre taped my ankle up. Our coach, Jean Perron played me in game one, game two, game three, game four and game five, and along with my awesome teammates that season, I accomplished a life-long dream of winning what many experts believe to be the hardest to win trophy in professional sport, the Stanley Cup. I was literally a couple of decisions away from missing my one chance at being part of a championship team.

And here's what haunts me to this day:

What if I hadn't found a way to stay **HUNGRY**?

References

Page 2–Kang, Lawler Albion, Mark, *Passion at Work: How to Find Work You Love and Live the Time of Your Life*

Page 8– homas, Evan, *Robert Kennedy- His Life*

Page 19–Butterworth, Eric, *You Make the Difference*, p105

Page 20–Maxwell, John, *Your Roadmap to Success*

Page 21-22–May, Rollo, *A Man's Search for Himself*, 1946 book, *Man's Search for Meaning*, Victor Frankl

Page 24– Ferrazzi, Keith, *Never Eat Alone*

Page 25–Johnston, Mike and Walter, Ryan, *Simply the Best: Players on Performance*

Page 25- Inamori, Kazuo, *A Passion for Success*, McGraw Hill Inc, 1995, p54

Page 27- Butterworth, Eric, *You Make the Difference*

Page 31–Kanter Moss, Rosabeth, *Confidence*

Page 34–Johnston, Mike and Walter, Ryan, *Simply the Best: Players on Performance*, Heritage House Publishing Company Ltd., p 74.

Page 44–Johnston & Walter, *Simply the Best: Insights and Strategies from Great Hockey Coaches*, 2004

Page 44–http://www.referenceforbusiness.com/management/Ex-Gov/Futuring.html

Page 45–Kiev, Dr. Ari, *A Strategy for Daily Living*

Page 47–http://www.1800gotjunk.com/ca_en/about/our_company.aspx

Page 50–Kouzes, James and Posner, Barry, *The leadership Challenge*, Josey-Base 2007 Wiley and Sons, p 28-31

Page 51–Buckingham, Marcus and Coffman, Curt, *First Break All the Rules; What the World's Greatest Managers do Differently*, 2003

Page 59–http://www.make-your-goals-happen.com/reticular-activating-system.html

Page 60–Siebolt, Steve, *Secrets of the World Class*

Page 60–Johnston, Mike and Walter, Ryan, *Simply the Best: Insights and Strategies from Great Hockey Coaches*, Heritage House Publishing Company Ltd.

Page 61 – Anderson, Mac, *The Power of Belief* © 2006 Unstoppable Enterprises Inc.

Page 62–Johnston, Mike and Walter, Ryan, *Simply the Best: Players on Performance*, Heritage House Publishing Company Ltd., p 18

Page 63-64–Elliott, John PhD, CD set *Maverick Mindset* Nightingale Conant

Page 65–McCain, John http://www.usnews.com/news/articles/2008/01/28/john-mccain-prisoner-of-war-a-first-person-account

Page 66–Johnston, Mike and Walter, Ryan, *Simply the Best: Insights and Strategies from Great Hockey Coaches*, Heritage House Publishing Company Ltd.

Page 67–Bennis, Warren *"Leaders" Strategies for taking charge*, Wallenda Factor,

Page 68–Johnston, Mike and Walter, Ryan, *Simply the Best: Insights and Strategies from Great Hockey Coaches*, Heritage House Publishing Company Ltd.

Page 72–Zander, Rosamund and Benjamin, *The Art of Possibilities*

Page 73-74–Zander, Rosamund and Benjamin, *The Art of Possibilities*

Page 76-78–Gilbert, Dr. Rob 2006 *Read this book tonight to help you win Tomorrow, Championship Performance*

Page 94–*Havard Business Review* September http://www.vtti.vt.edu/PDF/7-22-09-VTTI-Press_Release_Cell_phones_and_Driver_Distraction.pdf

Page 94–Bregman, Peter May 2009 *Harvard Business Review*, Two Lists You Should Look at Every Morning

Page 95-96–Collins, Jim 2003 (Dec 30) *USA Today* A "Stop Doing" List Best New Years Resolution

Page 97–Fairhurst, G. *The Art of Framing: Managing the Language of Leadership*, 1996.

Page 98-99–*Bell, Josh Violinist and the Washington Post* http://www.snopes.com/music/artists/bell.asp

Page 107–Cialdini, Robert, *Influence*

Page 111–Johnston and Walter, *Simply the Best: Players on Performance*, Heritage House Publishing Company Ltd.

Page 113–Kang, Lawler Albion, Mark, *Passion at Work: How to Find Work You Love and Live the Time of Your Life*

Page 114–Britton, Dan Page, Jimmy, *Wisdom Walks*

Page 120–Johnston and Walter, *Simply the Best: Players on Performance*, Heritage House Publishing Company Ltd.

Page 123–Butterworth, Eric, *You make the Difference*, p 27 Harold Russell Story

Page 125, Waitley, Dennis, *Allowing Setbacks to Spur You On*

Page 144–Clemmer, Jim, *Leadership Digest*

Page 148–*Gallup* A happy employee is a healthy employee, according to a GMJ survey, by Steve Crabtree reference for gallop study

Page 148–Buckingham, Marcus and Coffman, Curt, *First Break All the Rules; What the World's Greatest Managers do Differently*, 2003

Page 150–The Arbinger Institute, *Leadership and Self-Deception*, Berrett-Koehler Publisher, Inc., 2000

Page 151-152– *Gallup* Buckingham, Leadership Conference CD

Page 156–Butterworth, Eric, *You Make the Difference*, Study of Teacher

Page 157–Williams, Pat, *Coaching Your Kids to Be Leaders: The Keys to Unlocking Their Potential*, http://www.enotalone.com/article/3958.html Danny Rorebough

Page 172–Lencioni, Patrick, *The Five Dysfunctions of a Team*

Page 172–Joung,W., Hesketh, B., & Neal, A. (2006). "Using 'war stories' to train for adaptive performance: Is it better to learn from error or success?" *Applied Psychology: An International Review*, 55, 282-302

Page 174–Johnston, Mike and Walter, Ryan, *Simply the Best: Insights and Strategies from Great Hockey Coaches*, Heritage House Publishing Company Ltd., 265

STAY HUNGRY!

Are you inspired? Do you want to continue your *hungry* momentum? I have built a natural online extension at:

www.inspiringyourbestgame.com.

Inspiring your BEST GAME membership brings you a new two-minute inspiring video, article, and podcast every Monday morning. Your accumulated videos, articles, and podcasts are archived in your own personal console, accessible at any time. In addition I look forward to answering your questions at the Ask the Coach section of the website. *Inspiring your BEST GAME* is another way to feed your *hungry spirit* throughout the year to come.

Free Gifts!

Gift #1
To thank you for purchasing *HUNGRY! Fuelling Your Best Game*, I would like to offer you a gift. Please use the code hungry for 25% off the retail price of an Inspiring Your Best Game membership at:

www.hungryfuellingyourbestgame.com/gift

Gift #2
To thank you for purchasing *HUNGRY! Fuelling Your Best Game*, I would also like to offer you 25% off the retail price of a selection of my other books. Please use the code hungry for 25% off select books at:

www.hungryfuellingyourbestgame.com/gift

Gift #3

Thousands of people receive Ryan's e-newsletter, *Playing and Staying Hungry*, filled with tips on increasing performance, developing leadership and creating strong teams. You can sign up for FREE at:

www.hungryfuellingyourbestgame.com/gift

Do you want to share *HUNGRY! Fuelling Your Best Game* with others? Check www.hungryfuellingyourbestgame.com for volume discounts.

Ryan is Hungry to Coach your People!

Ryan has been working with companies, organizations, and teams for more than 20 years, helping them to feed, lead, and succeed in the areas of high performance, team, and leadership.

Using his *hungry* model, you and your people can experience significant growth and development in your Inner, Outer, and Team Games from Ryan's:

1. Keynotes - (banquets, conferences, sales meetings, leadership retreats)
2. Training - (half-day, full-day, multi-day experiential learning)
3. Coaching - (your top leaders in all of these touch points)

For more information please contact Ryan at:

info@ryanwalter.com

What Hungry Clients are Saying:

"While all of our speakers did a fine job your speech in particular was, to say the least, amazing. I am not exaggerating when I say that I got shivers going down my spine during your presentation. After listening to you I felt as if I could run through a wall."

Jagger Babuin,
The Personnel Growth and Development Corporation

"Ryan has an excellent stage presence and did a great job keeping the crowd engaged with his stories and important life lessons."

Steve Scholz,
Executive Director, Spartan Foundation

"I have been fortunate enough to hear many professional speakers in the same arena as Ryan and I can say that he is truly one of the best. My players are still talking about their time with Ryan and have implemented many of his suggestions. What Ryan has done for the Brown Men's Hockey Team is something that would be valuable to any organization."

Roger Grillo,
Head Coach Hockey, Brown University

What Fans Are Saying About Ryan's Other Books

Ryan One on One

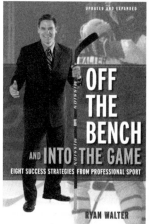

Off the Bench and Into the Game, which has sold more than 20,000 copies worldwide:

"Ryan takes the lessons learned from a life in hockey and shows you how to apply them for success in... family life, business life, journey of life. Corporations spend millions of dollars to train people in team building exercises that hockey teaches as part of the experience. This book is straightforward and honest, easy to read and will make you think. Ryan doesn't preach, he simply lays it out for you... I highly recommend it."

Tom McCauley
Monticello S & E,
Saint John NB, Canada

Ryan 2 on One, with Mike Johnston

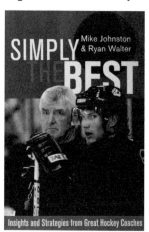

Simply the Best: Insights and Strategies from Great Hockey Coaches

"...The common thread that runs through all these top coaches is their ability to overcome adversity and failure, whether it was getting fired, getting blown out in a playoff series or struggling to make ends meet while learning their craft. The successful coaches are stubborn in their beliefs and goals, and years of experience also provide insights into motivating people. So this easy-to-read volume is an ultimately useful guide to budding coaches and anyone in the human potential industry."

–Canada Post, August 2009

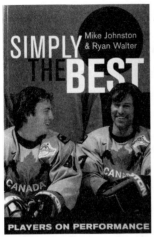

Simply the Best: Players on Performance

"What makes players simply the best? That's what coach Mike Johnston and former NHL great Ryan Walter set out to discover in *Simply the Best: Players on Performance*. The authors interviewed Sidney Crosby, Cassie Campbell, Shane Doan, Jarome Iginla, Ed Jovanovski, Trevor Linden, Scott Niedermayer, Joe Sakic and Hayley Wickenheiser to discover how they prepare to be the best in the world, how they lead a dressing room from the inside out, and how coaches best inspire their winning performances.

Young and old alike will be inspired and motivated as they gain access to exclusive insights directly from the players. *Simply the Best: Players on Performance* is not only a must-read for hockey fans, players and coaches, but will also resonate with anyone pursuing excellence, individually or as part of a team."

–Heritage House

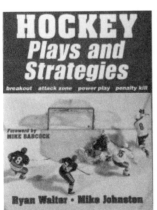

Hockey Plays and Strategies

"I am forever indebted to you and Mike Johnston for putting together one of the best educational hockey books I have ever had the pleasure of reading... a must have resource which I go back to again and again. It is a permanent fixture on my night stand."

Alex Hung
Vancouver, BC

Hockey Plays and Strategies is without a doubt the single best hockey strategy resource I have yet seen–anywhere. I read a lot of hockey books, manuals, digests and publications, etc. In the course of preparing for these CEP clinics... your methods and descriptions are by far the most comprehensive and well-described on the market. It pulled things together and allowed the reader to follow the game on paper the way you see it on the ice. A lot of books give you discrete plays and strategies, but I don't remember ever seeing them laid out with such continuity and clarity. Well done.

I credited you and your book in my recent CEP clinics and recommended *Hockey Plays and Strategies* to the coaches in attendance as the single best resource that I have seen on the subject.

David A. Baun, Esquire
Law Offices, BAUN & LITT,
Doylestown, Pennsylvania

Hungry Author

Ryan Walter's purpose and passion prompted him to play and coach more than 1100 games over 17 seasons in the National Hockey League. He was drafted second in the world, became the youngest NHL captain, won a Stanley Cup, played in the NHL All-Star Game, became a Vice-President of the National Hockey League Players Association, and was honoured as NHL Man of the Year.

After he was inducted into the BC Hockey Hall of Fame and the Burnaby Sports Hall of Fame, Ryan stuck to coaching his sons in minor hockey. During those years he obtained a Master of Arts Degree in Leadership/Business, co-founded two start-up companies in addition to his own, became a television hockey analyst, a hockey adviser and actor for both television and movies, invented a board game, and wrote 5 books.

Ryan is currently the Head Coach of the Canadian National Women's Hockey Team and a widely sought-after international speaker, interactive trainer, and leadership expert. From the ice, the bench, the podium, the page, and the screen his mission remains to *inspire the hungry spirit*.

www.ryanwalter.com

www.hungryfuellingyourbestgame.com

www.inspiringyourbestgame.com